Starting Statistics

E. L. Hanson, M.A. and G. A. Brown, B.SC.

GW00537864

HULTON EDUCATIONAL PUBLICATIONS

What this book is about

Starting Statistics

In this book you will be studying all the basic ideas on statistics.

Visual Statistics

We first show you how statisticians put the facts and figures into diagram form and later go on to show how pie charts, histograms and pictograms can be used to show data.

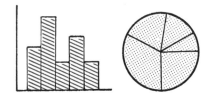

Derived Statistics

The next section of the book deals with statistics which are derived by calculations from the data. The most important of the derived statistics are the mean and standard deviation, partly because they are so closely related to the normal curve.

Probing Probability

We then introduce probability and some of you will no doubt be surprised to discover that probability is simple relative frequency and that you can use histograms, means and standard deviations to find out more about probability. We then discuss how you can use probability and sampling to test ideas by experiments.

Sampling

Up to this point the book has been about one variable and its frequency.

Regression

We now go on to show you a little about the statistics of two variables. You will be learning how to draw regression lines, find regression equation lines, find regression equations and how to measure correlation and rank correlations.

Correlation

We hope this book will help you to understand the ideas in statistics and that you will learn something about its uses and misuses.

Contents

Acknowledgements

We would like to express our thanks to the following C.S.E. Boards for permission to use examples from some of their past papers.

The Associated Lancashire Board, the Metropolitan Regional Board, the West Midland Board.

Thanks are also due to the following for permission to reproduce photographs and statistics:
H.M.S.O. Crown Copyright Division; Barnaby Picture Library; U.S.A. Information Service; Granada T.V.; Fox Photos; Sport & General Press Agency; *The Daily Express.*

© 1969
E. L. HANSON
G. A. BROWN
ISBN 0 7175 0176 0

First published 1969 by Hulton Educational Publications Ltd.,
Raans Road, Amersham, Bucks.
Reprinted 1971, 1972, 1975
Revised and reprinted 1977
Revised and reprinted 1983
Phototypeset by BAS Printers Limited, Wallop, Hampshire, England
and printed in Hong Kong by Wing King Tong Co., Ltd.

1 Starting Statistics

Statistics deals with ways of collecting and sorting out information and then drawing conclusions from this information.

The information can be about things or about people or what people do and say. Much of the information about people is collected through interviews or by questionnaires. Questionnaires are carefully made question-and-answer forms. They are used very widely because they are easy to make and seem easy to use. Later on you will find out that they may, in practice, be very unreliable.

As a simple example of collecting information, suppose someone wanted to know what you are carrying in your pockets today. If you agreed to tell them, what would you do? You would empty your pockets out on to the table, sort the things out into piles and then make a list of them.

Things carried in my pocket

Things (Variable)	Number of things (Frequency)	Things (Variable)	Number of things (Frequency)
Pennies	7	Penknives	1
Marbles	3	Ballpoint Pens	2
Compass	1	Bus passes	1
Sweets	8	Dinner Tickets	4
Photos	2	Combs	1

This list is called a **frequency distribution.** It tells us how many of each item we have collected.

Frequency means the number of items or facts collected.

The **variables** are the items or facts which are being studied.

This information could be put in a diagram which would be easier to read than a list. The second **block diagram** or **histogram** enables you to compare things quickly and show a lot of information clearly and in a small space.

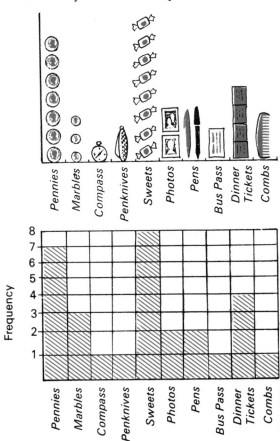

4

Having collected your things, sorted them out and drawn a diagram of your results, you can draw simple conclusions about them. For instance, you could say, 'I have more sweets than any other thing in my pockets.' Or 'I have twice as many dinner tickets as photos.' Or 'I have no screw-drivers in my pocket.'

Think of some other conclusions you can draw and express these conclusions in as many different ways as you can.

A statistician does an exactly similar job. He (1) collects the facts, called **data,** (2) sorts them out, (3) shows a diagram of them, (4) draws conclusions from them.

SOME OF THE JOBS STATISTICIANS DO

IN INDUSTRY
Firms interested in efficiency and good organization employ statisticians to plan the sampling of new materials and prod-ucts and to find out which ways of making things are most efficient.

IN MEDICINE
Statisticians analyse the effects of using new drugs to make sure they are safe and effective. They collect data on patients suffering from various diseases. Medical statisticians were the first to suspect that heavy cigarette smoking produces cancer.

IN SCIENCE
Data from experiments and observations in atomic physics, biology, space travel need very careful analysis. Recently statisticians have been studying the paths of space capsules to see how well they keep to the correct orbit.

IN GOVERNMENT
The Central Office of Information collects data on taxes paid, buildings erected, etc., so that the Government can make its decisions with all the facts before it.

1. Complete the following table of a traffic census carried out on the M.4 motorway between 9 a.m. and 9.05 a.m. Draw a histogram of the data. (‖‖ = 5. It makes counting easier.)

Vehicle	Tally score	Frequency
Motor cycles	‖‖ ‖‖	10
Cars	‖‖ ‖‖ ‖‖ ‖‖ ‖‖ ‖‖ ‖‖ ‖‖ ‖‖ 111	—
Lorries	‖‖ ‖‖ ‖‖	15
Coaches	‖‖ ‖‖ ‖‖ 1	16
Buses	‖‖	—
	Total =	—

2. Check on how many hours you spend in one school day in (*i*) work in school, (*ii*) homework, (*iii*) travelling, (*iv*) eating and drinking, (*v*) other personal needs, (*vi*) leisure, (*vii*) sleep. Draw a histogram of the data. Make sure the total number of hours is 24. Compare your histogram with a friend's and write a brief account of the differences between them.

2 Collecting and sorting data

When data has been collected, it has to be sorted out, reorganised and put into a readable form. In the last unit we used the simplest table of data, the frequency distribution. Below is a frequency distribution of the favourite colours of a group of pupils.

FAVOURITE COLOURS OF 36 PUPILS: FREQUENCY DISTRIBUTION

Favourite colour (Variable)	Red	Green	Blue	Yellow	Other Colours	Total
Number of pupils (Frequency)	12	9	9	2	4	36

Each of the colours (including 'other colours') is in a compartment of its own. We call each compartment a **class,** or in modern mathematics a **set.** We try to use fewer than ten classes so that the table is easy to read.

Sometimes we are interested in proportions or percentages so that we can compare different sized classes. To do this we make a **relative frequency distribution.** In this the proportion Red/Total, Green/Total and so on are shown.

$$\text{Proportion} = \text{Relative Frequency} = \frac{\text{Frequency of each class}}{\text{Total}}$$

The relative frequency can be written as a fraction, decimal or percentage. We prefer to use the last two since it is easier to compare decimals or percentages.

FAVOURITE COLOURS OF 36 PUPILS: RELATIVE FREQUENCY DISTRIBUTION

Favourite Colour	Red	Green	Blue	Yellow	Other Colours	Total
Relative Frequency	12/36 =0·33	9/36 =0·25	9/36 =0·25	2/36 =0·06	4/36 =0·11	36/36 =1·0

What should the total relative frequency always equal?
Add the relative frequencies given in decimal form.

Does your second answer differ from your first? If so, why?

6

Counting and Measuring

You can either count things or measure things. Counting and measuring things are the two basic methods of collecting data. You might count the number of people who like pop music. If you wanted to find out how popular a certain record is, you might count the number of people who liked it. If you wanted to find out how tall a person is you would measure him. All statistical information or data is found by either **counting** or **measuring.**

Data which we collect by counting things is called **discrete** data.

Data collected by measuring things is called **continuous** data.

Discrete data is the 'either/or' kind. Silver coins formed a good example. You could have either sixpences or shillings or florins or half-crowns (or occasionally crowns) and there were no silver coins in between these.

Continuous data can, in theory, have any value in a given range. For example, you can get married at any time from your sixteenth birthday to the time you die. So you could get married at the age of 19 years 6 months 1 week 2 days 14 hours 2 minutes 59·66 seconds. In practice no one would ever want that degree of accuracy. Instead we are more interested in whether a person was married between 18 and 19 years, or 19 and 20 years, or 20 and 21 years and so on. The ranges 18–19, 19–20, 20–21 are known as **class intervals.**

One has to be careful with class intervals. Suppose you get married on your nineteenth birthday. Would you be in the 18–19 class interval or the 19–20 class interval? To avoid argument we use the class interval 18–19 to mean: 'from the age of 18 years up to but *not including* the age of 19 years'. So if you were married on your nineteenth birthday, you would be in the 19–20 class interval.

1. Complete this table of shoe sizes for a group of 15 year old boys.

Size of shoe	3	4	5	6	7	8	9	10	11	Total
Frequency		2		4	10		5	4	2	40
Relative Frequency	0·025					0·25				1

Which shoe sizes are the most common?

2. The proportions of English girls with red, blonde, brown and black hair are estimated to be 5%, 14%, 60% and 21% respectively. In a group of 25 girls there are 19 girls with brown hair, 2 blondes, 3 with black hair and 1 redhead. Draw up a table and diagram to compare this group with the total population of English girls.

3. State which of the following represent discrete and which continuous data: (*i*) brands of beer, (*ii*) pound notes, (*iii*) incomes of teachers, (*iv*) sizes of shoes, (*v*) lengths of feet, (*vi*) scores from throwing two dice, (*vii*) colours of the rainbow.

4. The table below is a relative frequency distribution of incomes in a very large company.

Income (£'s)	3200–3999	4000–4799	4800–5599	5600–6399	6400–7199	7200–7999	8000–9999	over 10000	Total
Percentage earning this amount	17·2	11·7	12·1	14·8	15·9	11·9	12·7	3·6	

(*i*)   What is the usual class interval?
(*ii*) How many different class interval sizes are there?
(*iii*) In which class would the income £3999.50 be put?
(*iv*) What percentage earn less than £5599.50?
(*v*)   Why does the percentage total not equal 100% exactly?

3 Some facts about people in Britain

Here is a series of tables and charts of facts about the people of Britain. Each table or chart answers a simple question. Look at the data carefully and try to answer the questions.

1. How many people were there in 1971?

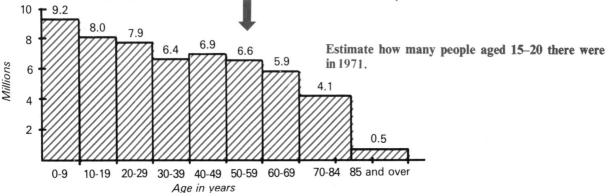

Estimate how many people aged 15–20 there were in 1971.

2. How many weddings?

What is the most probable age of marriage for men and for women?
Did as many men register their marriages as did women?

MARRIAGES IN BRITAIN IN 1979		
Age	*Men*	*Women*
Under 21	55,867	133,554
21–24	140,399	128,444
25–29	97,614	64,589
30–34	47,331	33,487
35–44	37,964	29,622
45–54	19,063	14,981
55 and over	18,689	12,250
Age not stated	—	—
TOTALS		

3. How many births?

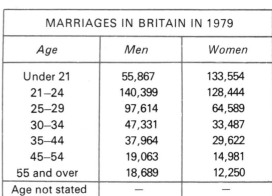

What does '30·91 babies per 1,000 women' mean?
What is the most common age for having children?

4. How many deaths?

DEATHS IN BRITAIN IN 1979													
Age (years)	Under 1	1–4	5–9	10–14	15–19	20–24	25–34	35–44	45–54	55–64	65–74	75–84	85 and over
Male (1000's)	5.45	8.748	0.708	0.707	2.042	1.969	4.012	6.868	21.83	56.94	110.17	96.03	32.10
Female (1000's)	4.03	0.62	0.43	0.46	0.70	0.74	2.24	4.54	13.67	33.27	75.61	118.86	80.84

How many men in the age range 75–84 years died?
Why did fewer people of 85 and over die than those between 75 and 84?
Do women live longer than men?

These charts were compiled from the *Annual Abstract of Statistics*. Statistics of life, births, weddings and deaths are called **vital** statistics. (This term 'vital statistics' was borrowed by newspaper men to refer to another different set of figures!)

5. How did people spend their money in 1979?

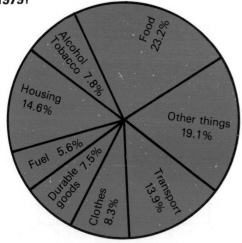

The percentage is the proportion of income spent on each item by the 'average' family.

How much would you expect a man earning £6,000 per annum to spend (a) on clothes, (b) on fuel? Would you expect every family to spend its income in these proportions? Give reasons for your answer.

1. Collect and tabulate the number of pupils who were born in each month of the year.
2. Collect, organise and tabulate the amount of pocket money each member of the class receives.
3. Draw a diagram to illustrate the figures in the table.
   If you were a manufacturer of household goods in 1965, which of the items would you concentrate on making? Why?
   Do the same percentages for 1965 and 1979 refer to the same population? Give reasons for your answer.

HOUSEHOLDS OWNING DURABLE CONSUMER GOODS		
	1965 %	1979 %
Television set	88	95·8
Washing machine	56	76·6
Refrigerator	39	92·9
Telephone	22	67·2

4 Showing data

Diagrams and graphs are used a great deal in statistics because, with a little practice, they are easier to read than tables of figures.

The most common graph is the **straight line graph.** The diagrams show two money conversion graphs. You might think you get more French francs than Danish Kroner for your pound. But notice the scales are different. The third graph shows the same information drawn to the same scale. Always look carefully at the scales—otherwise you may be misled.

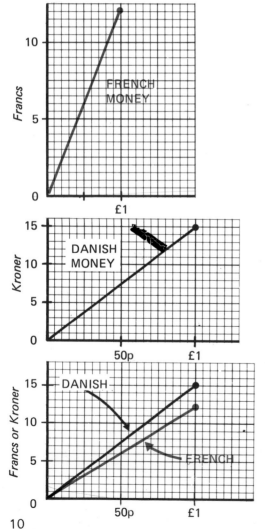

A continuous record of temperature changes is drawn by an automatic recording thermometer (above). The next graph shows the same data when only one reading was taken every hour. The points are joined with short straight lines. Because we cannot say that the temperature variations follow these lines exactly, the lines are 'broken' and we have a **broken line graph.**

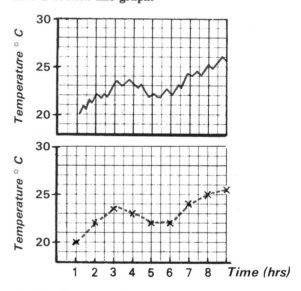

This diagram shows the sales of bathing costumes for a shop in Hounslow, Middlesex. It looks to be a declining business. But is this necessarily true? One always has to beware of graphs which show sales which are easily influenced by the weather or the time of year.

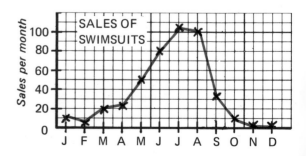

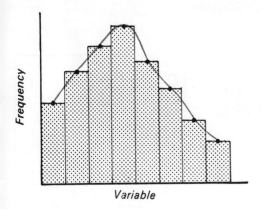

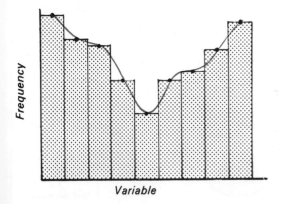

Above is the familiar histogram. When the columns are of equal width, their heights give you the frequencies or numbers of items recorded. If you join up the mid-points of the tops of the columns, you get the **frequency polygon.** This one is roughly bell-shaped. Not all histograms are bell-shaped. The one below is 'U' shaped.

Regional Population 1960

Estimated regional population 2000 AD

This diagram shows the number of people who were living in the different parts of the world in 1960 and how many will probably be living in these areas in the year 2000. The diagram uses pictures instead of columns. Such diagrams are called **isotypes.** They are easy to read, but can be misleading. What do you notice about the scale on this diagram?

All the graphs have been carefully labelled and the scales marked clearly. Many of the graphs and diagrams found in newspapers and propaganda pamphlets omit titles and have distorted scales. Sometimes this is done deliberately to cheat you so keep a look out for it.

1. The table gives the average number of houses built per month. Round the figures off to the nearest thousand and design an isotype chart using this symbol for 5,000 houses.

Country	Houses built per month
Western Germany	45,200
United Kingdom	29,494
Italy	14,786
Netherlands	5,707
Sweden	3,717
Denmark	1,942

2. A man spends $\frac{1}{5}$ of his wages on fares and meals, $\frac{1}{4}$ on household bills, gives $\frac{1}{2}$ to his wife and keeps the rest. Draw a circle of 1 inch radius and divide it into the above proportions and label them. Such a chart is known as a **pie chart.**

11

5 Distorted data

The diagrams and statements which follow are examples of statistics designed to mislead you. The names and firms used are, of course, purely fictitious.

Look at each diagram and statement carefully and write down (a) what the chart or statement is actually about, (b) what has been deliberately missed out or distorted to try and mislead you.

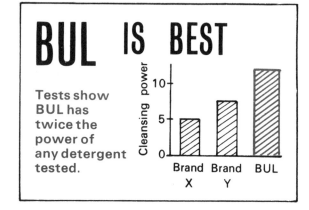

BUL IS BEST

Tests show BUL has twice the power of any detergent tested.

P.G.I. pops ARE TOPS!

P.G.I. pops were top money spinners. Sales manager Gordon Dumas says 'Record Sales have soared fantastically. We are easily in the lead'.
The figures speak for themselves.

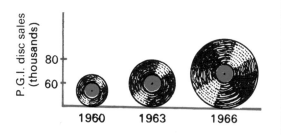

WHO WILL WIN AT MUDFORD ?

The Conserverals have strengthened their position in the last two elections and will easily beat the Socialatives.

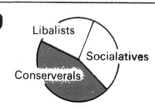
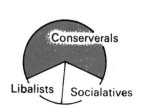

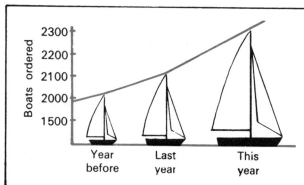

SALES SOAR AT BOAT SHOW

Statistics show boat sales have increased. The chart shows the number of boats ordered at the last three boat shows.

1. Collect examples of good and bad statistical charts from newspapers and compare them.
2. What are the common ways of distorting data?
3. Design an advertisement for either a new shoe cleaner or a new cosmetic and include some 'statistics' to support your claim for the product.
4. What is wrong with these statements?

SHORTAGE OF DENTISTS. The dental service is understaffed. Only 27·7% of the population received dental treatment last year.

WETTEST JULY IN EGYPT FOR OVER FIFTY YEARS. The rainfall was fantastic. The Egyptians talk about nothing else. It was 30 times that of any July since records were first kept 50 years ago.

OLD PEOPLE ARE GETTING YOUNGER. The average age of people in Blodwick's Old People's Home last year was 89. This year it is only 87.

NEWS FLASH!
Weeds are on the up and up ! ! !

Over 30,000 gardens inspected by our experts were found to be weed ridden.
We can solve your problems once and for all by F.I.R.E., the wonder weed killer.
Write to Box 14, East Fizley for details NOW.

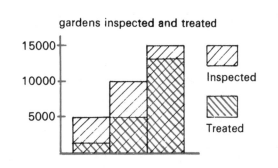
gardens inspected and treated

6 Cumulative frequencies

Look at the following tables. They give the marks of twenty-eight boys in a statistics test.

I.

Class interval (Marks)	Frequency (Number of pupils)
0– 9	4
10–19	6
20–29	8
30–39	6
40–49	4
Total	28

II.

Class interval (Marks)	Frequency (Number of pupils)
Under 10	4
Under 20	10
Under 30	18
Under 40	24
Under 50	28

The first table is a frequency distribution like those we have already studied. The second table gives exactly the same information, but in a different way. The class intervals get wider and wider as one goes through the table and the frequencies increase and increase. The frequencies accumulate. This table gives the **cumulative frequency distribution**. Notice that the final class interval of the cumulative frequency distribution is the same as the whole range of table I, and the total of 28 in table I is the same as the 'Under 50' frequency in table II. These are useful checks when one is changing a frequency distribution into a cumulative frequency distribution.

Table II is only one way of setting out a cumulative frequency distribution. Instead of 'under 20' and 'under 30', one could use '20 and under' and '30 and under'. A third way would be to use 'over 20' and 'over 30' and so on. **Can you think of a fourth way?**

The next table shows you a very close relation of the cumulative frequency distribution. It is known as the **relative cumulative frequency distribution,** which is quite a mouthful, so we shorten it to **R.C.F.D.** The relative frequencies can be written as fractions, decimals or percentages. Percentages are preferred because they are easy to compare and most people understand them.

Class interval (Marks)	Relative Frequency (Percentage)
Under 10	14·2
Under 20	35·7
Under 30	64·3
Under 40	85·7
Under 50	100·0

How are the percentages worked out?

Cumulative distributions and R.C.F.D's. can be plotted as curves. A normal or 'bell-shaped' distribution plotted as a cumulative frequency distribution gives a curve called an ogive. You will see an ogive drawn in the example on the opposite page.

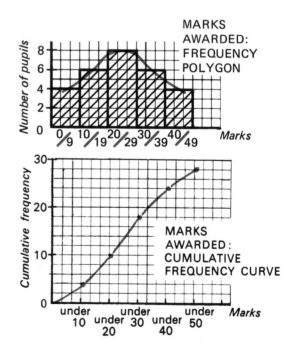

MARKS AWARDED: FREQUENCY POLYGON

MARKS AWARDED: CUMULATIVE FREQUENCY CURVE

Relative cumulative frequency distributions (R.C.F.D's) are used by examiners to find out what percentage of candidates pass and fail. The ideal distribution of marks for a large number of candidates is a bell-shaped curve.

Relative Frequency (%)

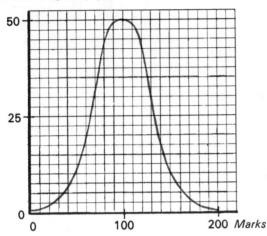

Relative Cumulative Frequency

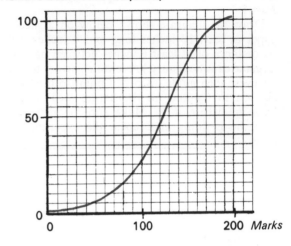

What percentage of candidates scored under 50 marks?

What was the range of marks for the middle 50% of the candidates?

1. Distinguish between 'under 15', '15 and under', '15 and over' and 'over 15'.
2. Look at the following tables and decide what is wrong with them.

Age started smoking	Cumulative Frequency
Under 12	10
Under 14	20
Under 16	18
Under 18	48

Number of football games attended	5 and under	10 and under	15 and under
R.C.F.	25%	40%	60%

3.

Hours of T.V. watching	0–5	6–10	11–15	16–20	21–25	Total
Number of people	25	45	60	45	25	200

The table gives the number of hours a sample of 200 people spent watching T.V. Convert the table into a cumulative frequency distribution and draw the cumulative curve. (Use '5 and under' etc.)
What is the shape of the R.C.F.D.?
How many hours do the first 50% of the sample spend watching T.V.?
What percentage of the people spend 18 hours or less watching T.V.?

7 An experiment on 'Knowledge of results'

The following experiment is to test the theory that a knowledge of results improves performance.

Part 1

Draw the diagram shown below on a sheet of paper at least 10 inches long and 8 inches wide. (A distance of at least 6 inches between base and target area is necessary.) Ask your partner to close his eyes; then guide his pencil point to the 'base'. He has to try and hit the 'target area' without knowing where it is. Make sure he never sees what he is doing and repeat the experiment 20 times.

Why were you asked to do the second part 21 times and not 20?

Why were you told to use a pencil and a ballpoint pen?

What was the most common hit in part 1 and in part 2?

What was the range of hits in part 1 and part 2?

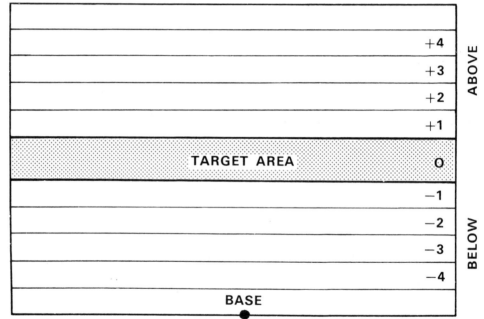

Part 2

Give your partner a short rest and then repeat the experiment using a ballpoint pen. After each try tell him exactly how far off target he was, e.g. '2 above', '1 below', etc. This time have 21 tries.

Group the results for the first part called 'No knowledge of results' and for the second part called 'Knowledge of results'. Plot histograms for the first and second parts.

Compare the two histograms and try to decide whether knowledge of results did improve your partner's performance. You can collect the results for the whole class and draw class histograms.

In the second part of the experiment described above you probably found that you had more hits concentrated on or about the target area. The number of hits on the target increased and the range of hits narrowed with a knowledge of the results.

You showed your results by drawing two histograms. Another way of doing it would be to find the averages and a measure of the spread of results for each part of the experiment.

The next sections deal with averages and measures of spread, how they are used and abused and how they can be calculated.

Examples I — Visual statistics problems

1. The height of each column of the histogram gives the number of 11 year old boys whose spending money is the amount at the foot of the column.

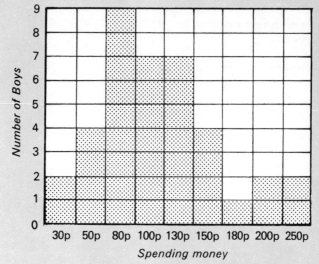

(a) What was the total number of boys in the sample given?

(b) What was the total spending money received by those boys who each got less than 130p spending money?

(c) What fraction of the sample received more than 80p but less than 180p?

2. Below are given a set of merit marks gained by a class during twelve weeks:

Week	1	2	3	4	5	6	7	8	9	10	11	12
No. of marks	5	4	5	8	3	10	6	9	7	10	6	8

(a) Draw a bar chart showing the cumulative total of marks at the end of each week.

(b) How accurately can the cumulative total at the end of Week 13 be estimated?

3. The following table shows the result of a survey to find the percentage of boys in a certain school who favour one sport more than any other:

Sport	Association Football	Rugby Football	Cricket	Swimming	Others	No Favourite
Percentage	45	20	15	10	5	5

(a) Represent these figures accurately by the areas of sectors on a circular chart, labelling the chart neatly.

(b) Write down the number of degrees in the angle at the centre of the sector representing rugby football.

(c) If the number of boys whose favourite sport is rugby football is 112, how many boys have cricket as their favourite sport?

4. The following table gives the number of deaths from scarlet fever during a certain year: Draw a histogram for the data. Combine the first three groups into one age group, i.e. less than 5 years. Show how this combination changes the histogram. What is the significance of the information lost by combining these age groups?

Age in Years	No. of Deaths
Less than 1	16
1	69
2– 4	237
5– 9	213
10–14	70
15–19	27
20–24	25
25–29	15
	672

5. The following marks were obtained by 48 students in a mathematics examination:

26	65	57	23	22	20	54	87
53	50	60	62	12	19	40	41
80	72	89	63	92	15	42	28
82	78	46	46	35	56	43	41
62	48	70	34	24	44	86	54
63	66	50	42	7	49	52	45

Prepare a table showing the frequency of marks for the ten class intervals 0–9, 10–19, 20–29, etc. For example: 1 student has a mark in the range 0–9, 3 students have marks in the range 10–19, and so on. From your results construct the histogram (or column graph) for this distribution.

6. The following table is a census of the size of shoes (neglecting half sizes) worn by the boys in a school.

Size of shoe	3	4	5	6	7	8	9
Totals for each size for the whole school	10	17	16	23	25	14	10

Draw the histogram. Explain briefly how a local shopkeeper who supplied the school with the shoes could make use of the census.

7. In one year, the average expenses for a company's cars were as follows:
   (i) Petrol £600
   (ii) Tax £80
   (iii) Insurance £120
   (iv) Repairs and Maintenance £280
   Show these facts as a pie chart.

8. The data opposite represent the average weekly output of passenger cars for each month of the year.
   Represent by means of a discontinuous graph the table opposite, and answer the following questions:
   (a) Which month had the greatest output of cars?
   (b) During which month was the least number of cars produced?
   (c) During which months was there a sudden increase in the weekly output? Comment on the reason for this.

Month	Production of passenger cars Weekly Average
January	8,251
February	4,480
March	6,415
April	8,000
May	7,894
June	7,229
July	8,300
August	7,321
September	7,670
October	8,231
November	7,782
December	7,002

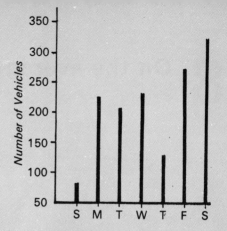

9. The table and column graph show the results of a traffic census taken in a one-way shopping street.

Day of week	S	M	T	W	T	F	S
Total number of vehicles	65	227	208	230	131	276	325

Draw out this answer table in your exercise book and complete it.

	Answer	Working (if necessary)
(i) How would you account for the decrease in traffic on Thursday?		
(ii) It is reckoned that 70% of the traffic passes between 8.30 a.m. and 6.30 p.m. How many vehicles (ignoring fractions) pass *outside* these hours on Friday?		
(iii) What is the drop in traffic between Saturday and Sunday calculated as a percentage of the total for Saturdays?		
(iv) Explain briefly why it is better not to join the tops of the columns in this particular kind of graph.		

10. (i) What were the 'takings' for the week?
    (ii) Why were Thursday's 'takings' low?
    (iii) Why were there no figures for Sunday?
    (iv) What percentage of the 'takings' were made on Saturday?
    (v) Is the above chart a histogram?

11. A man drives from London to Manchester. At the end of each hour he marks on a chart the distance travelled during that hour.
    (i) Why do you think he did only 65 kms. during the first hour?
    (ii) Why do you think he did only 30 kms. during the third hour?
    (iii) How did he manage to go 110 kms. in one hour?
    (iv) How long did the journey take him?
    (v) How far is it from London to Manchester?
    (vi) Would there be a better way of showing this information?
    (vii) Is the diagram strictly speaking a histogram?

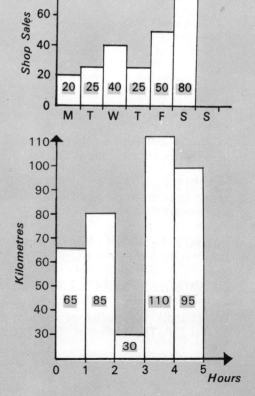

8 On the average

You often hear talk of 'the average man', 'the average smoker', 'the average wage', 'the law of averages' and 'on average'. What does the word 'average' really mean?

Averages are measures of the middle scores of distributions. There are three important averages which you need to know about.

Let us take a look at the wages of a firm of eight people. You might work out the average wage by dividing the total wage bill by eight. This gives £9250. But no one earns this actual amount.

Position in firm	Wages per year
Owner and managing director	£18,500
Accountant	£12,000
Secretary	£10,500
Chief Clerk	£9,000
4 assistants earning £6000	£24,000
Total wages bill	£74,000

Half the people get only £6000 each and the 'middle' wage is £7500. This is halfway between the fourth and fifth wages taken in order. All these figures are averages of different kinds.

£9250 is the arithmetic **MEAN. It is found by adding all the wages together and dividing by the total number of people.**

£6000 is the **MODE. It is the most common or most frequently occurring wage.**

£7500 is the **MEDIAN. It is found by putting the wages in order and finding the middle value.** For example, the median of £5, £15, £20, £25, £100 is £20. The median of 100, 200, 220, 400 is 210.

Means, modes and medians are all 'averages'. Whenever you read about an average ask yourself which average is really meant.

Which average do you think the Managing Director would use if the assistants wanted more money?
Which average do you think the assistants would use?
Which is the fairest?

All the averages on their own can be misleading as you will see from the following examples.

The Mean

The mean wage in each factory is £80, the range of wages is the same, but the distribution of wages is very different. The mean is the only average which is based on every single wage. Knowing the mean and the total number of employees one can work out the total wages bill.

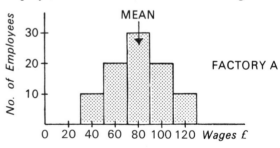

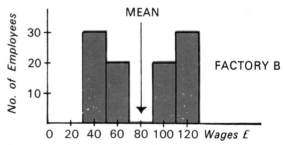

What are the total wage bills in factories A and B?
What other way of finding the total wages bill can you think of?

The Mode

The modal wage in both factories is £75. The range of wages in the two factories is the same, but again the distribution is different. The mode can be found very quickly. On its own it does not give you a clear picture of the wage structure. It only uses a fraction of the data.

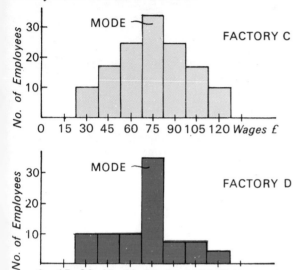

In which factory would you rather work?

The Median

The median splits the employees into two equal groups. The median wage in factory E is £75.

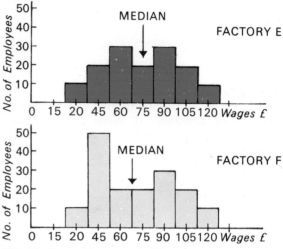

What is the median wage in F?

Notice that although the medians split the distribution in half the two halves can be very different.

The median is fairly easy to work out.

How many people work in each factory?

The conclusion is that if you want a fair picture of the wages you need to know more than the 'average' wage. You want to know which average it is and a measure of the spread of wages and the distribution.

1. Find the mean, mode and median of the following sets of figures:
   (a) 1, 1, 3, 5, 7, 9, 11, 13.
   (b) 1001, 1002, 1002, 1003, 1004.
   (c) 27, 36, 21, 48, 21, 17.
   (d) £105, £117, £118, £105.
2. Try and decide which average is being used in the following statements:
   (a) The average size of shoe is 8.
   (b) The average family contains 2·2 children.
   (c) The average smoker consumes 25 cigarettes a week.
   (d) The average pupil scored 40%.
3. Find the mean values of the following:
   (a) £5000; £6000; £6500; £30000.
   (b) 4·01, 4·03, 4·05, 4·06. 4·07, 4·12 metres.
   (c) 5,3,6,5,4,5,2,8,6,5,4,8,3,4,5,4,8,2,5,4.
   Can you see easy ways of doing these calculations?
4. Four groups consisting of 15, 20, 10 and 15 girls have mean weights of 45 kg, 53 kg, 54 kg, and 49 kg respectively.
   What is the mean weight of the whole group?

9 Calculating the mean

The table and histogram give the amount of money spent by a group of girls in one week on tights. The amounts are given to the nearest 25 pence. How can we calculate the mean amount spent?

FREQUENCY TABLE

Number of girls	Amount spent
10	50p.
5	75p.
2	£1.00
5	£1·25
10	£1·50
Total = 32	

HISTOGRAM

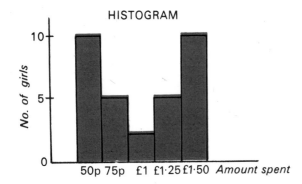

You can easily see from the histogram that 10 girls spent 50p each, 5 girls spent 75p each and so you can easily find the total amount spent. The mean amount is found by dividing the total amount by the total number of girls.

The best way of setting out the calculation is to put it in a table like the one shown.

CALCULATION TABLE

Column I No. of girls	Column II Amount spent	Col. I × Col. II
10 5 2 5 10	50p. 75p. £1 £1·25 £1·50	10 × 50p. = £5 5 × 75p. = 2 × £1 =
Total girls =		Total money =
Mean amount spent =		

Set the table out in your book and complete it.
What was the mean amount of money spent?
Which column gives you the frequency?
Which column deals with the variable?
Why do we not add up column II?

1. The table gives the number of goals scored by a local team in 30 matches. Find the mean number of goals scored per match.

Goals	0	1	2	3	4	5
Number of matches in which these goals were scored	4	8	6	5	4	3

2. In one particular week the amount of money spent by each group of tight-buying girls mentioned above was doubled.
   Calculate the mean amount for this particular week and draw a histogram of the new amounts spent.
   How does it compare with the histogram shown?
   What would happen to the mean if the amounts spent were halved?

Using an arbitrary zero

There are five student-teachers whose heights are 185 cm, 173 cm, 178 cm, 188 cm, and 191 cm. What is their mean height? You could work it out in the usual way. Total height is 915 cm, divide by the total number of people, i.e. 5, and the mean height is 183 cm.

Or you could take 180 cm off each height (which is the same thing as letting 180 cm be the zero of the height scale) and then the new heights would be + 5 cm, − 7 cm, − 2 cm, +8 cm, + 11 cm.

The total of the new heights is 15 cm, so the mean is 15/5 = 3 cm on the new scale. The true mean is then 180 + 3 = 183 cm, which is what we got before. This last step is very important. If you don't do it you would get the mean height of the student-teachers to be 3 cm!

We can sum this up by saying that in this example we used 180 cm as the arbitrary zero, worked out the mean on the new scale and then converted back to the old, true scale.

Mean on true scale = Arbitrary zero + Mean on new scale.

3. Ten measurements of the diameter of a metal cylinder were recorded as: 5·18, 5·19, 5·23, 5·41, 5·36, 5·11, 5·12, 5·42, 5·36, 5·1 12 centimetres. What is the 'best' estimate of the actual diameter of the cylinder?

4. Find the mean age of the following ten children using an arbitrary zero.

Bert 10 yr. 9 mth.	Harry 10 yr. 6 mth.	Charlie 10 yr. 7 mth.
Isaac 10 yr. 0 mth.	Derek 11 yr. 0 mth.	John 11 yr. 1 mth.
Fred 10 yr. 5 mth.	Keith 10 yr. 5 mth.	George 9 yr. 11 mth.
Larry 10 yr. 4 mth.		

10 Further ways of finding the mean

In the last unit you learnt to calculate the mean in two ways: from a frequency table and using an arbitrary zero. In this unit you will learn another two ways of finding the mean. Both of them are based on frequency distributions.

Look at the table of marks given below and try to decide how the figures in each column were arrived at. Complete the table and find the mean.

MARKS OF FORM 5A			
Marks Class interval	Frequency (F)	Class Mid- Values (m)	(F) × (m)
1– 5 6–10 11–15 16–20 21–25	5 10 15 10 5	3 8 — — —	5 lots of 3 = 15 10 lots of 8 = 80 15 lots of 13 = — 10 lots of — = — — — — — = —
	Total frequency = 45		Total Marks = 585

$$\text{Estimated mean} = \frac{\text{Total Marks}}{\text{Total Frequency}} = \frac{585}{45} = 13$$

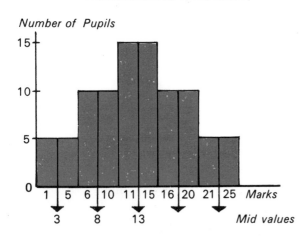

Number of Pupils

Mid values

Why do we use the middle value of the class interval? Why is the answer called the estimated mean?

The final method of calculating the mean makes use of the idea of class mid-values and also uses the new scale based on an arbitrary zero. To make the method easier to understand we shall use the figures given in the first example.

Try to decide how the figures in the fourth column are arrived at.
Complete the fifth column. This gives you the total marks on the new scale.
Find the mean mark on the new scale.
Then you can find the mean mark on the original scale.

Class Interval	Frequency (F)	Class Mid-value	New Scale Mid-value (s)	(F) × (s)
1– 5	5	3	0	5 × 0 = 0
6–10	10	8	1	10 × 1 = 10
11–15	15	13	2	15 × 2 = 30
16–20	10	18	3	— × — = —
21–25	5	23	4	— × — = —
	Total frequency = 45			Total marks = 90

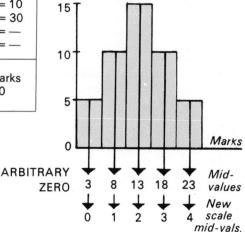

The arbitrary zero is 3.
5 units on the original scale
= 1 new unit.

Total marks (new scale) = 90
Total frequency = 45

Estimated mean (new scale) $= \frac{90}{45} = 2$

We must now multiply this new scale figure by 5 to convert it back to the original scale, estimated mean on new scale = 10

$$\underset{\text{true scale}}{\text{Mean on}} = \underset{\text{zero}}{\text{Arbitrary}} + \underset{\text{new scale}}{\text{Mean on}}$$
$$13 \quad = \quad 3 \quad + \quad 10$$

As before the estimated mean works out to 13.

What is the advantage of this last method?
What would the new scale mid-values be if the arbitrary zero was 13?

1. The heights of 100 male university students are given in the table. Obtain the estimated mean height.

Height in centimetres	152–158	159–165	166–172	173–179	180–186
Frequency	5	18	42	27	8

2. (a) Measure the heights of the members of the class. Group the data in class intervals of 5 cm and obtain the mean height and the range of heights.
   (b) What does the estimated mean height become if the class intervals are widened to 10 cm?
   (c) Which is the more accurate estimated mean height, answers (a) or (b)? Give a reason for your answer.

3. Complete the following table based on sales by tobacconists.

Value of sales	Number of tobacconists (F)	Class Mid-value	New Scale Mid-value (s)	(F) × (s)
£1,000– £2,500	1,200	1,750	0	1,200 × 0 = 0
£2,500– £4,000	900	3,250	1	900 × 1 = 900
£4,000– £5,500	700	4,750	2	700 × 2 = 1,400
£5,500– £7,000	500	6,250	—	— × — = —
£7,000– £8,500	250	7,750	—	— × — = —
£8,500–£10,000	50	—	—	— × — = —
	Total = frequency			Total = sales

(a) What is the arbitrary zero?
(b) How many units of the original scale equals 1 new unit?
(c) What is the estimated mean value of sales of tobacco?

25

11 Measuring spread

After they had played in ten cricket matches both Mr. Hanson and Mr. Brown had a mean score of fifty runs. Which of them is the steadier batsman? Unless you know more about the range or spread of their scores you cannot give the answer to this question. In fact their scores in the ten matches were:

| *Mr. Hanson* | 41 | 44 | 47 | 54 | 55 | 48 | 50 | 53 | 49 | 59 |
| *Mr. Brown* | 0 | 35 | 50 | 50 | 65 | 20 | 30 | 100 | 80 | 70 |

Mr. Hanson is a much steadier cricketer. (He says this is because he comes from Lancashire.) His scores are in a narrow range. Mr. Brown's scores are widely spread. But both have the same average (mean score) of 50 runs. **Check this.**

Whenever one is describing data, one needs to give an average (and say which one it is) and a measure of the spread or range of the data. This gives a fair picture of the data and does not mislead people. The examples on page 20 show you how misleading the average can be on its own.

Not long ago a small survey of *The Times* newspaper readers was carried out and the mean salary of a *Times* reader was found to be approximately £6000. So you might think, 'It's no use my reading *The Times*: it's only for rich people'. In fact the range of salaries of *Times* readers is from £0 (students) to over £100000 per year (chairmen of big businesses). Also more students read *The Times* than do the chairmen of big businesses. **Why is this?**

The Measures of Spread

There are four measures of spread. They are **(1) The range (2) The interquartile range (3) The variance (4) The standard deviation.**

The range. This is **the lowest score to the highest score.** For example, the range of Mr. Hanson's scores is 41 to 59, which is 18. **What is the range of Mr. Brown's scores?**

As you can see, the range is very easy to find but it only uses two items, the top and bottom ones, and leaves out the rest. This makes it a very crude measure.

The interquartile range. This is the name for **the middle 50% of the scores.** This is usually found from the cumulative frequency curves of the data. There is an example on the opposite page. Sometimes cumulative frequencies are expressed in percentages. The cumulative frequencies are then called **percentiles.** If you were told your mark was at the 25th percentile you would know you were a quarter of the way up the mark list (in order of merit). **How far up the mark list would you be if your mark was at the 75th percentile?**

The interquartile range is from the 25th percentile to the 75th percentile. Since it uses 50% of the original data, you get a fairer picture than the one you get from just the range.

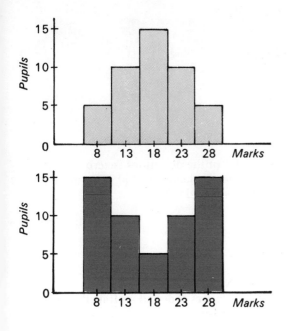

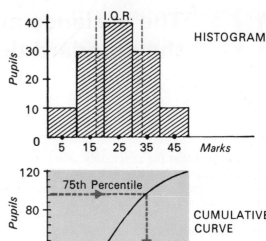

THE RANGE

The histograms show two possible sets of marks for a class. The range of marks is the same in both cases. Yet the distributions are very different.

What are the class intervals?
What are the mean marks?
Estimate the means from the histograms.

THE INTERQUARTILE RANGE

The dotted lines in colour show the middle 50% or interquartile range.

The second diagram shows the cumulative frequency curve of the marks in the first diagram.

Finding the interquartile range (I.Q.R.) is easier using the cumulative curve.

Estimate the I.Q.R. from the diagrams.
What is the range of marks?

---

1. The table gives the marks of 200 pupils in History and Mathematics. Find the interquartile range and the median mark in both subjects. (Hint: use the cumulative frequency curves.)

	MARKS					
Subject	0–9	10–19	20–29	30–39	40–49	Totals
History	10	30	70	60	30	200
Mathematics	35	40	50	40	35	200

Which is the easiest subject to pass in if (*a*) the pass mark in both subjects is 25, (*b*) the pass mark in both subjects is 35?

2. In a certain city in India the drainage system designed by British engineers in the nineteenth century was based on the mean annual rainfall in that area. What important fact did the engineers not take into consideration?

3. Obtain the deviations (differences) of Mr. Hanson's scores from his mean score of fifty and add them together. Do the same with Mr. Brown's scores. What conclusion do you draw about the total deviations from the mean?

12 The variance and the standard deviation

You have seen that the range only uses two items and the interquartile range only uses 50% of the items when measuring spread. What we really want is a measure of spread which uses all the items. One way might be to take all the deviations (differences) from the mean and add them together. But, as you saw in Question 3 in the last section, if you do this the answer is always zero.

To avoid this some statisticians wanted to ignore the plus and minus signs (just as some schoolboys do!) But after a time they agreed that ignoring signs was against the rules of mathematics, so they had to find another way.

If you want to stick to the mathematical rules and make all the signs of the deviations the same, then you must square each deviation. The squares of positive and negative quantities are both positive; you should know why this is so.

This is what statisticians do:

(1) **They find the deviations from the mean.**
(2) **Then square each deviation.**
(3) **Add the squared deviations together.**
(4) **Find the mean of the squared deviations.**

The total of the deviations is zero. The total of the deviations squared is 140. The mean of the deviations squared is 20.

The short name for the mean of the deviations squared is the VARIANCE.

VARIANCE =
$$\frac{\text{Total of squares of deviations from the mean}}{\text{Total number of items}}$$

Sometimes this is written in the shorthand form:
$$\text{Var.} = \Sigma \frac{(x - M)^2}{n}$$
Σ = total of, x = each item, M = the mean and n = the number of items.

The variance uses every item, but it has one serious disadvantage: it always gives an answer in squared units. If you are measuring lengths the variance is in lengths squared (or areas). If you are measuring times in hours, the variance is in

Here is an example:

Number (x)	Mean (M)	Deviation (x − M)	Deviation squared (x − M)²
10	17	−7	49
12	17	−5	25
15	17	−2	4
18	17	+1	1
20	17	+3	9
21	17	+4	16
23	17	+6	36
Total = 119 Mean = 119/7 = 17		Total = 0 A useful check	Total = 140 Mean = 140/7 = 20

squared hours (which hasn't really got a meaning). To avoid this snag of squared units, statisticians use the square root of the variance. This 'de-squares' the squared units and brings them back to the original units.

The square root of the variance is called the **STANDARD DEVIATION.**

The standard deviation = the square root of variance.

$$\text{STANDARD DEVIATION} = \sqrt{\frac{\Sigma(x - M)^2}{n}}$$

In the worked example the variance was 20. So the standard deviation is $\sqrt{20} = 4.45$.

The standard deviation is the most important measure of spread because it uses every item and is in the same units as the original data. The bigger the spread, the bigger the standard deviation. The mean and the standard deviation go together. They both use all the items. The mean gives the centre of the distribution, the standard deviation gives a measure of the spread of the distribution.

1. Find the standard deviation of both Mr. Hanson's and Mr. Brown's cricket scores.

2. Find the standard deviations for the following sets of figures:
   (i) 0 1 2 3 4 5 6 7 8 9
   (ii) 0 0 1 1 2 2 3 3 4 4 5 5 6 6 7 7 8 8 9 9
   (iii) 0 0 0 1 1 1 2 2 2 3 3 3 4 4 4 5 5 5 6 6 6 7 7 7 8 8 8 9 9 9
   What happens to the standard deviation in (i) if 10 is added to each figure?
   Hint: Use part (i) to find the answers to part (ii) and (iii).

3. Below are the results of a survey carried out in two towns on money spent in buying portable black and white television sets.

	Mean cost	Standard deviation
Town A	£71	£5
Town B	£65	£10

   Which town probably has the most expensive sets?
   Which town probably has the least expensive sets?

4. Find the standard deviation of:
   1 1 1 2 2 2 3 3 4 4 5 8·
   Can you find another way of doing the calculation using a frequency table as we did for the mean on pp. 20–21?

5. 15 babies were born in a maternity ward of a hospital. Their weights in grams were:
   272, 274, 278, 278, 281, 284, 286, 289, 292, 295, 297, 298, 300, 302, 309.
   Find the mean weight of the babies and the standard deviation.
   Hint: What arbitrary origin would make your calculation easier?

13 Why the standard deviation ?

Some people are puzzled by the standard deviation and ask, 'Why do statisticians use it?'

We have given you some of the reasons already. It uses every item of data. The range and the I.Q.R. do not. It is in the same units as the original data. The variance is not in the same units.

But the most important reason for using the standard deviation as a measure of spread is that it is related to a very common frequency distribution called the **NORMAL** or **BELL-SHAPED** distribution. Question 4 of Unit 12 was based on a normal distribution. Opposite are some more diagrams of normal distributions and the next section is devoted to them.

If you know (1) that a given distribution is normal, (2) the value of the mean, and (3) the standard deviation, then the following results are always true.

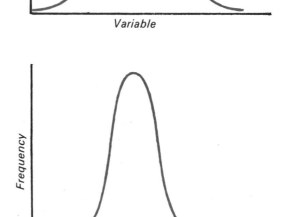

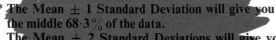

* The Mean $\pm$ 1 Standard Deviation will give you the middle 68·3% of the data.
The Mean $\pm$ 2 Standard Deviations will give you the middle 95·4% of the data.
The Mean $\pm$ 3 Standard Deviations will give you the middle 99·7% of the data.
The Mean $\pm$ $\frac{2}{3}$ Standard Deviation will give you the middle 50% of the data.

* For general use the approximate values of 68% and 95% are good enough.

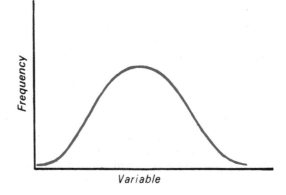

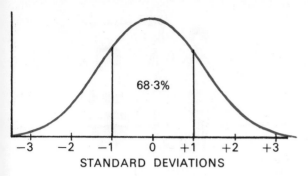

68·3%

STANDARD DEVIATIONS

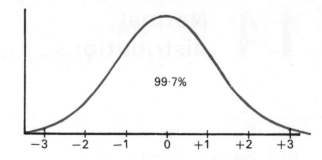

99·7%

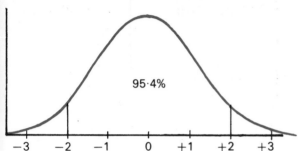

95·4%

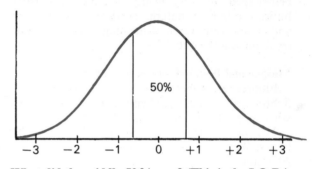

50%

An example: an accountant found out the following facts about the wages paid by a particular firm. The mean wage was £4000. The standard deviation was £550. The wages were normally distributed.

He was then able to work out the following facts:

68% of the workers earned £4000 ± £550; that is between £3450 and £4550.

95% of the workers earned £4000 ± 2 × £550; that is between £2900 and £5100.

99·7% of the workers earned £4000 ± 3 × £550; that is between £2350 and £5650.

What did the middle 50% earn? (This is the I.Q.R.)
What is the safest guess of the range of wages?
What percentage earn more than £5650?
What are the chances of earning more than £5650 in this firm?
What is the most common wage?

You can see that by just knowing three simple facts, the mean, the standard deviation and that the distribution is normal, you can work out a very clear picture of the original data. Similarly, if you want to describe a set of marks, or wages, or weights in the best mathematical shorthand, then you should use the mean and the standard deviation, and say if the distribution is normal.

1. The mean height of 1,000 guardsmen was 1·800 metres. The standard deviation was 2 centimetres. Assuming the heights of guardsmen are normally distributed find:
   (*i*) The approximate range of heights.
   (*ii*) The I.Q.R.
   (*iii*) How many guardsmen you would expect to find over 1·804 m tall.
   (*iv*) How many of the guardsmen were between 1·800 m and 1·804 m tall.
2. The wages paid in a factory were normally distributed and a shop steward discovered the I.Q.R. was £3200 to £4700. Work out as much as you can about the wages of the workers in this factory.
3. Intelligence is measured in units called Intelligence Quotients (I.Q.) The mean I.Q. of children in this country is 100, the standard deviation is 15 and I.Q's. are normally distributed.
   What percentage of children have an I.Q. of 145 and over?
   What is the interquartile range of I.Q.?
   What are the chances of having an I.Q. of 130 or more?

14 Normal distributions

Many frequency distributions are normal or bell-shaped, or very nearly so. Normal distributions occur in nature, everyday life, science and engineering. Look at the diagrams below and try to answer the questions.

Making and Testing Fluorescent Tubes

Fluorescent tubes are the cheapest form of lighting. They are filled with a gas which glows when an electric current passes through it.

The mean life of fluorescent tubes is 1,800 hours. The standard deviation is approximately 40 hours.

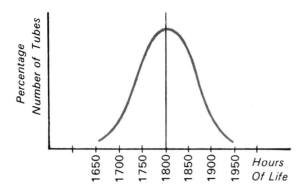

What percentage of the tubes will last less than 1,680 hours?
Do the manufacturers test the life of every tube they make?

Hand Spans

The hand spans of a group of adults is shown at the top of the next column. The left-hand diagram is of their 'strong' hand and the right-hand diagram of their 'weak' hand. The scales and units are the same in the diagrams. The actual figures have been omitted.

Are these statements TRUE or FALSE?
More people in this group have the same size of strong hand than of weak hand. In general people's strong hand is slightly larger than their weak hand.

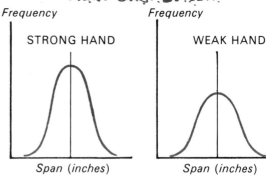

Knees and Skirts

Fashions change from year to year. In 1900 it was bold for a girl to show her ankles. In the 1920's skirts were worn at knee level. In the 1960's it was fashionable to wear skirts above the knee. Now in the 1980's the mini skirt is again fashionable.

Below is the distribution of skirts about the knees for a sample of girls aged 17–20 in 1966.

The distribution is nearly normal.

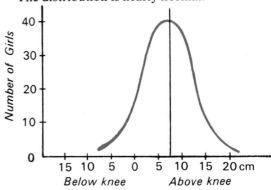

What is the most common height of skirt above the knee in this sample?
Are there more girls wearing skirts over 12.5 cm above the knee than there are girls wearing skirts below the knee?

Are Girls More Intelligent Than Boys?

The diagram shows the distribution of Intelligence Quotients for boys and girls. The distribution of intelligence is almost the same.

If you split I.Q.'s into different abilities, you find girls are slightly better at talking and writing and boys are slightly better at mechanical and spatial problems.

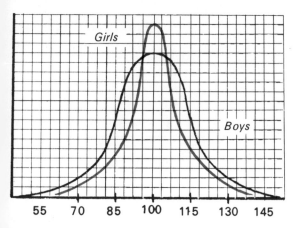

What is the mean I.Q. of boys and girls?
Are girls more intelligent or less intelligent than boys according to this diagram?

Standard Power Packs

When scientists are doing important research they need very precise instruments. Often they check the instruments several times and work out the mean reading and standard deviation.

Below are the results of checking two power packs. They should give 5 volts.
Which is the more reliable?

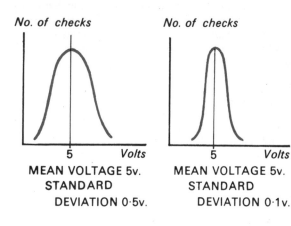

MEAN VOLTAGE 5v.
STANDARD
DEVIATION 0·5v.

MEAN VOLTAGE 5v.
STANDARD
DEVIATION 0·1v.

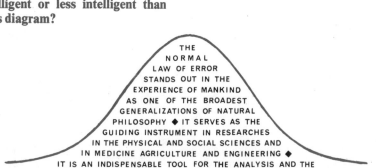

THE NORMAL LAW OF ERROR STANDS OUT IN THE EXPERIENCE OF MANKIND AS ONE OF THE BROADEST GENERALIZATIONS OF NATURAL PHILOSOPHY ◆ IT SERVES AS THE GUIDING INSTRUMENT IN RESEARCHES IN THE PHYSICAL AND SOCIAL SCIENCES AND IN MEDICINE AGRICULTURE AND ENGINEERING ◆ IT IS AN INDISPENSABLE TOOL FOR THE ANALYSIS AND THE INTERPRETATION OF THE BASIC DATA OBTAINED BY OBSERVATION AND EXPERIMENT

From W. J. Youden's *Elementary Statistical Methods*, Henry Holt 1943.

1. Collect the class results in the Knowledge of Results experiment (page 16). Draw frequency polygons for the conditions 'No Knowledge of Results', and 'Knowledge of Results'.
   Compare the frequency polygons. Are they approximately normal?

2. Here is a normal distribution of marks. The mean is 50 and the standard deviation is 10.
   What will happen to the distribution (*a*) if 10 is added to every mark, (*b*) if every mark is doubled?
   Sketch your answers.
   What happens to the mean and the standard deviation?

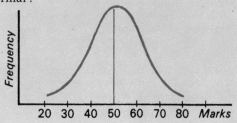

15 Moving averages

The table shows the attendances at the Saturday home games of a football team. The directors of the club wanted to know if attendances were declining so they plotted the attendances on a graph.

Home game	1	2	3	4	5	6	7	8	9	10
Attendance (*to nearest 500*)	12,000	10,000	11,000	11,000	9,500	8,500	12,000	9,500	10,000	12,000

There was so much variation in the attendances that the directors could not decide whether they were increasing, decreasing or staying fairly steady. So they called in a statistician to help them.

ATTENDANCES AT HOME GAMES

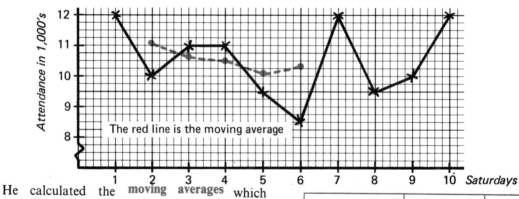

He calculated the **moving averages** which smooth out a lot of the variation and leave the general trend. He then plotted the moving averages on the same graph as the attendances and left the directors to decide whether or not they were declining. The first five moving averages are shown on the graph.

Here is part of the calculations of the moving averages for batches of three games at a time. Look at the table first to see if you can work out what the statistician did and then check with the instructions.

Attendances	Moving total in batches of 3	Moving average in batches of 3
12,000		
10,000	33,000	11,000
11,000	32,000	10,670
11,000	31,500	10,500
9,500	29,000	9,670
8,500	30,000	?
12,000	30,000	?
9,500	?	?
10,000	?	?
12,000		

To calculate the moving average of batches of three games:

(1) Find the total and average attendance for the first three games. The attendances were 12,000; 10,000; 11,000.
Total = 33,000
Average = 11,000

(2) Then find the total and average attendance for the next three games.
Total = 32,000
Average = 10,670

(3) Continue until you reach the end of the table.

The moving average is always placed at the middle point of each batch.

Complete the moving average table and plot the results on the graph. Find also the total average and plot this. What was happening to the attendances?

Moving averages are used whenever one wants to smooth out excessive variations in a set of data so that one can see the general trend. Strictly speaking, the moving average technique should only be used on countable (discrete) data.

Moving averages are used by a wide variety of people. Managers of big stores use them to find the trends in sales of clothes. Factory managers use them to see if daily (or weekly) output is tending to increase or decrease. Government departments use them to find out if exports are increasing or the 'balance of payments' is improving.

Sometimes moving averages are used to forecast future sales or output. This can be a very risky business. We leave you to decide why.

1. The graph shows the sales of football boots by a sports shop.
Can you explain the rise and fall in sales?
Work out the four-monthly moving averages and plot them.
Is it safe to say that sales are on the increase?

2. The table of export figures (far right) was issued by the Govt. of Panonia. Round the figures off to the nearest 100 million and plot the data and the three-yearly moving averages for the years 1974–1984.
Are exports steadily increasing?
Estimate the exports for the year 1985.
(The figure given in the table for 1985 is for January to July only.)
Hint: Using 3,000 million as an arbitrary origin eases the arithmetic and graph work.

3. These two tables give the exports of a certain country over a period of six years.
Mr. Brown wrote to a newspaper complaining that exports were declining and quoted his figures to prove it.
Mr. Hanson wrote in reply that exports were increasing and quoted his figures to prove it!
Who was correct and why?
(Draw the graph of these figures and their moving averages.)
Hint: Use a two-yearly moving average.

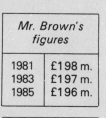

Mr. Brown's figures	
1981	£198 m.
1983	£197 m.
1985	£196 m.

Mr. Hanson's figures	
1982	£200 m.
1984	£210 m.
1986	£220 m.

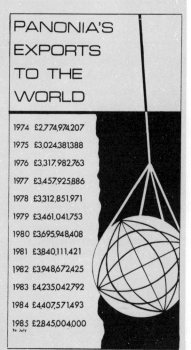

PANONIA'S EXPORTS TO THE WORLD

1974	£2,774,974,207
1975	£3,024,381,388
1976	£3,317,982,763
1977	£3,457,925,886
1978	£3,312,851,971
1979	£3,461,041,753
1980	£3,695,948,408
1981	£3,840,111,421
1982	£3,948,672,425
1983	£4,235,042,792
1984	£4,407,571,493
1985	£2,845,004,000
To July	

16 Weighted averages

If you buy 2 kg of expensive tea costing 480p per kilogram and 5 kg of cheap tea costing 200p per kilogram and mix them, what is the average cost per kilogram of the mixture? Most of you can work out the answer to this question. It is 280p per kilogram. This sort of question is called by statisticians a **weighted average** question.

A statistician would set out this problem using the weights of the cheap and expensive teas as follows:

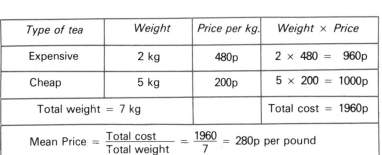

Type of tea	Weight	Price per kg.	Weight × Price
Expensive	2 kg	480p	2 × 480 = 960p
Cheap	5 kg	200p	5 × 200 = 1000p
Total weight = 7 kg			Total cost = 1960p
Mean Price = $\dfrac{\text{Total cost}}{\text{Total weight}} = \dfrac{1960}{7}$ = 280p per pound			

What would the average cost of the mixture be if you used 5 kg of expensive tea and 2 kg of the cheap tea? Set out your answer in the same way.

The meaning of 'weight' in statistics

The word *weight* in statistics has three meanings

(1) It can mean ordinary weight—tonnes, kilograms, grams, etc.

(2) It can mean *relative proportion*. In the above examples the relative proportions of the cheap and expensive teas determine the cost of the mixture.

(3) It can mean *how important?* You may have heard the phrase 'Old So-and-so attaches more weight to homework than anything else'. This does not mean Old So-and-so hangs weights on people's homework. What does it mean?

An example of 'How Important?'

Some big companies nowadays give their engineering apprentices short tests in Mathematics, Physics and English. One company considers Mathematics three times as important as English and Physics twice as important as English. So they 'weight' the marks in Mathematics, Physics and English as 3, 2 and 1 respectively. This means the Mathematics mark is multiplied by 3, the Physics mark by 2 and the English mark by 1. The total of these marks is found and this is divided by 6. (3 + 2 + 1 = 6)

The marks of two apprentices are given in the tables. We have worked out the first apprentice's 'weighted average mark' for you. Try to follow how we have done the calculations and then work out the second apprentice's weighted average mark.

Which apprentice obtained the better weighted mark?

FIRST APPRENTICE'S MARKS			
Subject	*Marks*	*Weight*	*Weight × Mark*
Maths.	50	3	3 × 50 = 150
Physics	60	2	2 × 60 = 120
English	78	1	1 × 78 = 78
Total weight = 6		Total = 348	
Weighted average mark $= \dfrac{348}{6} = 58$			

SECOND APPRENTICE'S MARKS			
Subject	*Marks*	*Weight*	*Weight × Mark*
Maths.	55	3	
Physics	60	2	
English	70	1	

What were the apprentice's crude average marks?

Weighted and Moving Averages Combined

Space capsules tend to wander off course slightly. When this happens a message is received from the capsule by a computer which then transmits a radio signal to the capsule to bring it back on course. But by the time this has happened the capsule is on a slightly different course so again needs correcting. This whole process of "Message–Correction signal—Message–Correction signal" continues throughout the flight of the capsule.

The most recent information on the capsule's actual course is obviously the most important and so most weight is attached to it. A message one second old is weighted $\frac{1}{2}$ the current message, a message two seconds old is weighted $\frac{1}{4}$ the current one and so on. The calculations are done at lightning speed by the computer which then transmits the correction signal to the capsule. The averages are weighted in favour of the current messages. The calculation of averages is always moving through the data so the computer is using the Weighted and Moving Averages combined.

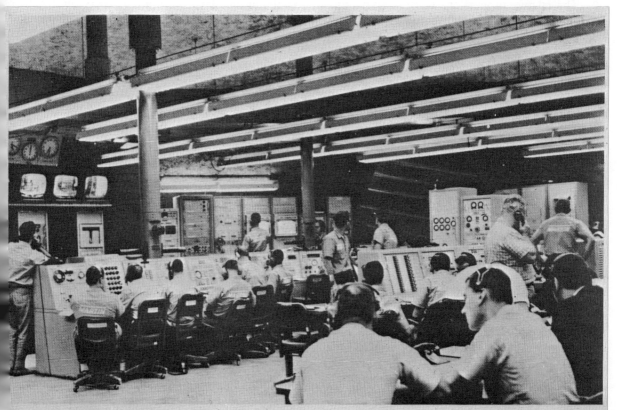

1. A Managing Director wanted a first rate private secretary. He decided to assess the girls who applied on a seven-point scale from −3, which means 'poor', through 0, which means 'average', to +3, which means 'very good', on certain qualities which he weighted. The first three applicants' results are given in the table. Which of them was offered the job?

QUALITY	WEIGHT	Miss Carlisle	Miss Mann	Miss Wood
Personality	1	0	2	3
Sense of humour	2	1	3	0
Experience	2	1	−1	−2
Accurate shorthand and typing	4	2	3	2
Social skill	5	1	2	1
Efficiency	5	2	3	2

2. The relative proportions of the populations of Puddleton and Drydollop are given below together with the deaths which occurred in each age group during the last year. Work out the weighted average rate of deaths per thousand for the two towns. Find also the crude (or simple) average rate of deaths per thousand. Which is the fairer average to use when comparing the two towns and why?

PUDDLETON. TOTAL POPULATION 150,000		
Age range	Relative proportion (Weight)	Deaths
0–10	30%	50
10–55	50%	300
55 and over	20%	900

DRYDOLLOP TOTAL POPULATION 210,000		
Age range	Relative Proportion (Weight)	Deaths
0–10	10%	50
10–55	40%	400
55 and over	50%	800

Examples II—Derived Statistics Problems

1. A wholesaler sold sacks of carrots containing approximately 40 kilograms in each sack. In fact, the weights of 15 of the sacks (to the nearest 250 gram) were:

   40·50 kg, 41·25 kg, 40·00 kg, 39·25 kg, 40·50 kg, 39·75 kg, 41·00 kg, 39·50 kg, 40·25 kg, 40·00 kg, 40·75 kg, 39·50 kg, 41·50 kg, 40·50 kg, 39·50 kg.

   Write down the positive or negative deviations of these weights from the advertised weight in lbs. Calculate
   (*i*) the mean weight, and
   (*ii*) the median weight.
   Why is there no modal weight for these sacks of carrots?

2. The weights of 10 sacks of potatoes are:

   50·20 kg, 50·70 kg, 50·75 kg, 50·90 kg, 51·50 kg, 49·80 kg, 50·70 kg, 50·25 kg, 50·30 kg, 50·60 kg.

   Make separate lists of these weights, approximated
   (*i*) to the nearest kilogram.
   (*ii*) to the nearest kilogram below.
   Calculate the mean of each of these lists of weights.
   Calculate the true mean of the original weights.
   For each of the approximate means, calculate the percentage error, correct to two places of decimals.

3. The following table shows the height of 100 recruits reporting to an army depot. From these figures draw the frequency polygon and the histogram of the heights of the men.

Height in centimetres	Frequency
152–155	1
155–158	3
158–161	5
161–164	8
164–167	18
167–170	21
170–173	17
173–176	12
176–179	7
179–182	5
182–185	2
185–187	1

   What do you understand by (*a*) mode, (*b*) mean? Calculate their values for these figures.

4. The sales of pairs of sheets in a store over a period showed the following distribution in price paid:

£10.50 to £12.90	...	...	24
£13.00 to £15.40	...	...	26
£15.50 to £17.90	...	...	26
£18.00 to £20.40	...	...	30
£20.50 to £22.90	...	...	40
£23.00 to £25.40	...	...	34
£25.50 to £27.90	...	...	14
£28.00 to £30.40	...	...	5

Draw a histogram for this distribution and construct a frequency polygon. Find the medial and modal class.

5. This question refers to the graph below. It shows the number of private cars passing along a toll road in each of the hours from 7 a.m. to 7 p.m. on a certain day. Each square represents one car, so that, for example, six cars passed between 8 and 9 a.m.

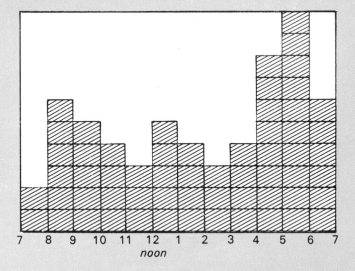

State whether the following are *true* or *false*:
(*i*)   The total number of cars in the twelve hours was 60.
(*ii*) The average (arithmetic mean) number of cars per hour was 6.
(*iii*) The average (mode) number of cars per hour was 10.
(*iv*) More cars passed before noon than after.
(*v*)   If the cost of operating the road and toll gates is about £6 per day, and each car pays 13p to pass along the road, the owners of the road will make a profit.

6.

Marks	No. of Pupils
0– 9	12
10–19	20
20–29	30
30–39	25
40–49	13
	100

Draw a cumulative frequency distribution of the above data and estimate the median and inter-quartile range.
If the pass mark was fixed at the 45th percentile, how many pupils passed and what was the pass mark?

7. The marks scored by a group of ten children in an examination were as follows:

56, 76, 39, 84, 64, 74, 48, 24, 42, 93.

What is the 'range' of these marks?
Calculate
(i)   the mean
(ii) the standard deviation for this set of results.

8. A certain distance was measured by each member of a group of children, with the following results:

Measurement in metres	8·8	8·9	9·0	9·1	9·2	9·3	9·4	9·5
Number of children	7	17	4	18	1	2	0	1

Find the arithmetic mean of these measurements and also the mean deviation from the arithmetic mean.

9. The contents of fifty boxes of matches of the same make were found to be as follows:

Number of matches	42	43	44	45	46	47	48
Number of boxes	10	6	20	6	5	2	1

Find the average number of matches in a box and the standard deviation.

10. The following table gives the number of cars completed by a certain firm in each quarter of the years 1961–64:

	First quarter	Second quarter	Third quarter	Fourth quarter
1961	360	428	412	420
1962	396	432	424	428
1963	404	460	444	464
1964	428	516	484	524

Make a table showing the four-quarterly moving average.
Draw in the same diagram a graph showing the quarterly numbers and a graph of the four-quarterly moving average.
Use the latter graph to estimate the total number of cars to be completed in 1965.

11. The figures below are the mean and standard deviations of wages in two petrol companies:

Pet Petrol   Mean £80   Standard Deviation £5 per week.
Troll Gass   Mean £70   Standard Deviation £7.50 per week.

(a) If foremen receive the highest wages, which firm pays its foremen most?
(b) Which firm pays its lowest paid workers least?
(c) What percentage of employees earn over £85 in Pet Petrol and Troll Gass?

17 Practical probability

I'M PROBING PROBABILITY SIR!

A teacher asked a large group of students to tell him the colour of their eyes. 150 of the 300 students had blue eyes, 96 had brown eyes and 54 had grey eyes.

We can say that $\frac{150}{300}$ students had blue eyes; or, to put it in a simpler way, we can say that $\frac{1}{2}$ the group had blue eyes.

We also have two other ways of saying the same thing.
(*i*) The **chances** of having blue eyes in this group are 1 in 2.
(*ii*) The **probability** of having blue eyes in this group is $\frac{1}{2}$.
Both statements mean the same thing, but mathematicians prefer to use *probabilities* because they are written in fraction or *ratio* form and so they are easy to add or multiply.

We can write in the following way the probability of having blue eyes in the group of students mentioned above:
Pr (Blue Eyes) =
$$\frac{\text{Number of people with blue eyes}}{\text{The total no. of people in the group}}$$

What is the PROBABILITY of having brown eyes in this group?

You can see now that *probabilities* are *relative frequencies*. (See Unit 2.) Like all relative frequencies they may be expressed as fractions, decimals or percentages.

The teacher in the above example found out the *probability* of one of his students having blue eyes by counting those with blue, brown and grey eyes. In other words, he found out by a *practical* method. Most probabilities in everyday life and in science are found in this way.

You may have read in newspapers such statements as these:

(*i*) IT RAINS ONE DAY IN THREE IN THE LAKE DISTRICT.
(*ii*) ONE IN EVERY 600 CARS STOLEN FROM CENTRAL LONDON.
(*iii*) 98 OUT OF 100 DENTISTS DISSATISFIED WITH THEIR JOBS.

Each of these statements is a *probability* statement in disguise. In statistical language the first statement reads:
Pr (days of *recorded* rain in Lake District) $= \frac{1}{3}$.

To find this out, the statistician took a count of the number of days in the last 5 years on which it had rained in the Lake District. He then divided this by the total number of days, 1826. In practice it was not quite as simple as this: the statistician had to decide whether to ignore slight showers. He also knew that he could give only a crude measure because there are only a few rain stations in any area, and it is possible that there was rain in the Lake District but not at the rain stations. In addition, the probability of $\frac{1}{3}$ does not take into account the variability of rainfall at different times of the year: in early September it might not rain at all, but in late November there might be continuous rain. You will see that simple *probabilities* can be only very crude measures, but they are useful for conveying information quickly.

The third statement said that 98 out of every 100 dentists are dissatisfied with their jobs. This was based on a survey of dentists in England and Wales, but only some dentists were sent the questionnaire and only some of these dentists bothered to reply. So we cannot say that the newspaper headline is completely true. What is true is that 98% of the dentists who replied said they were dissatisfied with their work. It might be that mostly dissatisfied dentists replied; or perhaps the questions were badly worded.

Below are two ways of asking a question which could produce the answer that the vast majority of dentists are dissatisfied with their work. Try to decide what is wrong with the design of the question.

1. Are you *ever* dissatisfied with your work? (*Answer* **Yes** *or* **No**)

2. Some dentists are dissatisfied with their work. Would you say that you were (a) never satisfied, (b) occasionally dissatisfied, (c) rarely dissatisfied, (d) never dissatisfied?

Can you make up better questions on work satisfaction?

Whenever you read a probability statement in a newspaper you should always ask yourself the question: How did they find that out? If the basis for the figures they give is not clear, then it is safer not to believe the statement.

How do you think the second statement on stolen cars was arrived at?

To sum up:

PROBABILITIES are relative frequencies. Simple probabilities are crude but useful measures. Always consider critically how the data was collected.

1. The following figures are based on actual motor-cycle accidents involving other vehicles, property and pedestrians.

Cars	Pedestrians	Walls and hedges	Cyclists	Lorries	Other motor cyclists	Buses
125	105	85	75	55	30	25

Draw a histogram of the data.
If you have a motor-cycle accident, what is the probability of (*i*) crashing with a car, (*ii*) running into a wall or hedge?
Why are there more crashes with cars than with lorries?

2.

from **THE DAILY SHOCKER**

from **THE MORNING SENSATION**

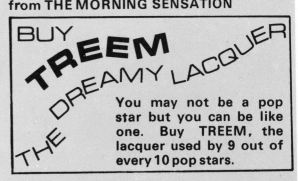

ONE IN TWO PEOPLE IN LONDON DO NOT BATH!

Surveys show that 1 in 2 people in London has not had a bath for over a year. So be careful: the person next to you in a London bus may be very dirty.

BUY **TREEM** THE DREAMY LACQUER

You may not be a pop star but you can be like one. Buy TREEM, the lacquer used by 9 out of every 10 pop stars.

Look at the above statements carefully and try to decide (*i*) what is wrong with the statements, (*ii*) what else you would need to know before you believed them.

18 Some experiments in probability

Here are some simple and interesting experiments in probability.

Coin Tossing Experiments

(H = head   T = tail)

1. One person tosses a coin 'fairly' 50 times and records the number of heads and tails in a table.
2. Two people each toss a coin 50 times and record their combined tosses.

(1)

H	T	Total

(2)

HH	HT	TT	Total

(3)

HHH	HHT	HTT	TTT	Total

3. Three people each toss a coin 50 times and record their combined tosses.

Collect the results for each experiment from the whole class and draw histograms of the results.

1. What is the practical probability of getting 3 heads using 3 coins, 2 heads using 2 coins and 1 head using 1 coin?
2. What is the practical probability of getting only 2 heads using 3 coins, 2 heads or less using 3 coins, no heads at all using 3 coins?
3. Find the ratio of the height of the heads-tail column to the height of the heads column in the histogram for Experiment 2.
   Give your answer to the nearest whole number.
   Give a possible reason for your answer.
4. What is the ratio of the probabilities of getting 2 heads and 1 tail to getting 3 heads in Experiment 3?

Dice Rolling Experiments

1. One person 'fairly' rolls a die (singular; plural *dice*) 60 times and another person records the number of times a 6 is obtained and not obtained.
2. One person rolls two dice 60 times and another person records the number of double sixes, single sixes and no sixes at all.
3. One person rolls three dice 60 times and another person records the number of treble sixes, double sixes, single sixes and no sixes at all.

(1)

Sixes	Not sixes	Total

(2)

Double sixes	Single sixes	No sixes	Total

(3)

Treble sixes	Double sixes	Single sixes	No sixes	Total

Collect the results for each experiment from the whole class and draw histograms of each set of results.

1. What is your class's practical probability of getting a six with 1 die, two sixes with 2 dice, three sixes with 3 dice?
2. Shade in the areas of the histograms which give the probabilities of getting one or two sixes with 2 dice, of getting two or more sixes with 3 dice, of getting one or two or three or four or five with 1 die. What are the practical probabilities given by these shaded areas?
3. What is the practical probability of getting one six with 2 dice, of getting two sixes with 3 dice?
4. What are the practical probabilities of not getting a six with 1 die, not getting a six with 2 dice, not getting a six with 3 dice?
Can you find an approximate rule connecting your three answers?

You can use *spinning tops* instead of coins or dice. They are easy to make and a group of people do not make as much noise using tops as they do tossing coins. You must make sure the shaft goes through the centre of the disc otherwise you get a biassed top.

Shaft off centre

Is the probability of getting 6 with this top increased or reduced?

Flicking Matchsticks

On a sheet of plain paper draw a series of parallel lines as wide apart as a matchstick is long.

One person flicks a match in the air above the paper and another records whether it lands across a line or between the lines.

Collect the results for the experiment from the whole class and work out (as a fraction) the probability of a match falling across a line.

Turn the fraction upside down, change it into a decimal and multiply it by two.

Do you recognise the answer? You could 'go round in circles' guessing what it should be!

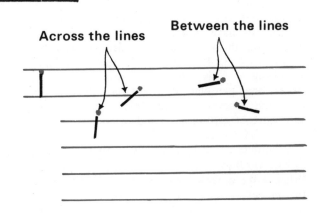

Across the lines   **Between the lines**

19 Theoretical probability

In the last unit you found probabilities by experiment. Instead of doing an experiment you could work out all the possibilities in theory. For instance, if you toss a coin it is bound to come down either heads or tails. So there are only two possibilities. The probability of getting heads is *one* possibility out of *two* possibilities. We could write this:

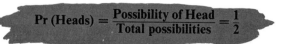

$$\text{Pr (Heads)} = \frac{\text{Possibility of Head}}{\text{Total possibilities}} = \frac{1}{2}$$

This method of working out possibilities we call the 'theoretical' method.

It is usually very easy to work out the possibilities, but you have to be sure that all the possibilities have equal chances of happening. When you throw a die there are six possible scores: 1, 2, 3, 4, 5 and 6. So the probability of getting a '5' is 1/6. But if you play with a professional gambler he might have loaded the die so that it never comes down a '5'. So you have no chance of getting a '5' and the probability of so doing is 0/6 which is 0.

A gambler could load the die so that '3' comes down every time.

What is the probability of getting a '3' using this loaded die?

Theoretical and practical probabilities are very closely related. The more results of experiments you take the nearer you get to the theoretical probability. Always providing the experiments have been carried out properly!

For example, in simple theory, the probability of getting 'Heads' in coin tossing is 1/2 or 0·5. In practice if you toss a coin over 10,000 times you are likely to get the probability of 'Heads' as 0·499. The head of a penny is raised and is slightly heavier than its tail. Over a long run the penny tends to land slightly more times on its head than on its tail.

Similarly, in simple theory, the probability of a baby being born a boy is 0·5. You might think therefore that the same number of boys and girls are born. In practice slightly more boys are born than girls. In 1960, 404,150 boys and 380,855 girls were born in England. The practical probability of a baby being a boy based on these figures is 0·515.

The Probability Scale

We have talked enough about probability for you to understand how it can be measured and calculated. Now we want to introduce you to 'The Probability Scale'.

If you toss a penny in the open air it is **absolutely certain** to come down again. We call this a probability of **1**. It is the highest point on the probability scale.

If you toss a penny in the open air it is absolutely certain that it will **never** come down a half-crown, no matter how often you try. We call this a probability of **0**. It is the lowest point on the probability scale.

All probabilities can be written as proper fractions or decimals and **all probabilities are between 0 and 1**. The probability scale is a way of helping you to remember this. If you get an answer which is outside the range 0 to 1, then either you have made a mistake or someone may be trying to cheat you.

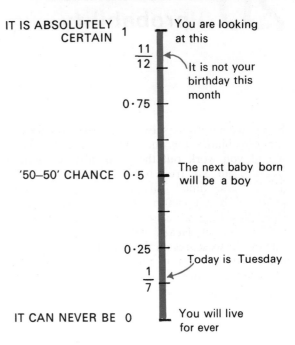

THE PROBABILITY SCALE

IT IS ABSOLUTELY CERTAIN — 1 — You are looking at this

$\frac{11}{12}$ — It is not your birthday this month

0·75

'50–50' CHANCE — 0·5 — The next baby born will be a boy

0·25

$\frac{1}{7}$ — Today is Tuesday

IT CAN NEVER BE — 0 — You will live for ever

What is the probability that:
(a) It is winter?
(b) It is your birthday today?
(c) Your Mother is older than you?
(d) You are the youngest in the class?
(e) Your desk will walk?
(f) You can swim to New York?

---

1. What is the probability of drawing from a pack of cards (a) the King of Hearts, (b) an Ace, (c) a Spade?

2. What is the probability of drawing from a bag containing 5 white and 4 black balls (a) a white ball, (b) a black ball, (c) at least one white ball if 5 balls are drawn from the bag at once?

3. A bookmaker gave these odds for a race at Ascot:

   Nimrod 6–1   *Peter Snow* 3–2   *Araby* 8–1   *Gone with the Wind* 7–4   *Go Fast* 2–1

   Odds give the chances of losing to the chances of winning. Thus *Nimrod* according to the bookmaker has six chances of losing to one chance of winning. The probability based on these odds of *Nimrod* winning is 1/7.

   $$\text{Pr}\,(Nimrod) = \frac{1 \text{ winning chance}}{6 \text{ losing chances} + 1 \text{ winning chance}} = 1/7$$

   Similarly *Peter Snow's* probability of winning is 2/5.
   Work out the probabilities for the other horses and find the total probability for the race. What peculiarity do you notice about the total probability?

47

20 The laws of probability

So far we have only shown you how to work out the possibilities for one coin or one die. How would you work out the probability of getting 'Heads' and 'Six' from tossing a penny and a die at the same time? This looks a more difficult problem, but it can be made easy by using a **Possibility Table** which sets out all the possibilities.

You can get 'Heads' with the penny and any one of the six scores on the die, or 'Tails' with the penny and any one of the six scores on the die. You can see from the table that there are therefore only 12 possibilities.

	⚀	⚁	⚂	⚃	⚄	⚅
HEADS	H1	H2	H3	H4	H5	H6
TAILS	T1	T2	T3	T4	T5	T6

Now 'Heads' and 'Six' together is only one of 12 possibilities and so the probability of throwing 'Heads' and 'Six' is 1/12.

Pr (Heads,Six) = 1/12

The possibility table shows that in order to find the total number of possibilities all you have to do is to multiply the number of possibilities of each separate event together.

Number of possibilities with coin × Number of possibilities with die = Total possibilities of coin and die together.

Another way of looking at the same problem of the probability of getting 'Heads' and 'Six' at the same time is as follows:

Probability of 'Heads' = 1/2
Probability of 'Six' = 1/6
Therefore probability of 'Heads' and 'Six' together = 1/2 × 1/6
= 1/12

You simply multiply the probabilities together in this sort of problem.

Written more shortly, the solution would be:

Pr (Heads) = 1/2   Pr (Six) = 1/6
Pr (Heads,Six) = 1/2 × 1/6 = 1/12

What is the probability of getting 'Heads and Six' OR 'Tails and Five'? Some of you may rightly guess the answer is 1/12 + 1/12 which is 1/6.

Pr (Heads,Six) = 1/12   Pr (Tails,Five) = 1/12
Pr (Heads,Six OR Tails,Five) = 1/12 + 1/12
$\qquad\qquad\qquad\qquad\qquad\quad = 1/6$

In this sort of problem you simply add the probabilities.

These two simple problems illustrate the **Laws of Probability.**

The first one in which you multiplied the probabilities together is an example using the **Multiplication Law** which states:

If the probabilities of two independent events are p and q, then the probability of both events happening is $p.q$.

Getting 'Heads' on the coin does not affect in any way the chances of getting 'Six' on the die, so we say that these two events are *independent* of each other.

The second problem in which you added the probabilities together is an example using the **Addition Law** which states:

If the probabilities of two exclusive events happening are p and q, then the probability of one or other of the events happening is $p + q$.

It is easy to remember when to multiply probabilities and when to add them. **Multiply** probabilities when the events **could** happen at the same time.
Example: What is the probability of getting two Heads when two coins are tossed?
Pr (Heads) for first coin = 1/2
Pr (Heads) for second coin = 1/2
Pr (Heads,Heads) $= \frac{1}{2} \times \frac{1}{2} = 1/4$

What is the probability of getting three Tails with three pennies?

ADD probabilities when the events **COULD NOT** happen at the same time.
Example: The probability of getting a Four OR a Five with the same die is 1/6 + 1/6 = 1/3

What is the probability of drawing any King or any Jack from a pack of cards?

Here is the possibility table for two dice. Use the table to answer the questions. Those of you who can handle 'Sets' could write your answers in set notation. Two sets are shown in red.

1. What is the probability of
    (a)   double six
    (b)   a total of 4
    (c)   a total of 1
    (d)   a total of 7 or 11
    (e)   a total of 9 or more
    (f)   a total of 7 or less
    (g)   not getting a total of 8
    (h)   not getting under 4?

2. Draw a histogram of the possible scores using 6 cm = a frequency of 6 and 2 cm as the width of each column of the histogram. What is the area of the histogram? What is the modal score?

49

21 Some examples in probability

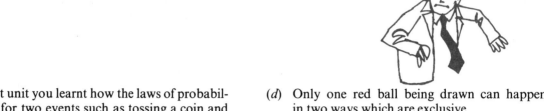

In the last unit you learnt how the laws of probability work for two events such as tossing a coin and rolling a die. Some of you may have guessed that the laws of probability also apply to three, four or even more events.

Below are some worked examples. Read the question carefully, spend a few minutes trying to do the question and then look at the way we have set out the answers. In this way you will quickly learn how to solve probability problems.

Example 1
A man has 4 black and 5 red balls in a bag. Without looking in the bag he takes out a ball, replaces it in the bag and takes out another ball. What is the probability that he:
(a) **gets two red balls**
(b) **gets a red ball and then a black ball**
(c) **gets a black ball and then a red ball**
(d) **gets only one red ball?**

Let Pr = probability. R_1 = first ball is red. B_1 = first ball is black etc.
M.L. = Multiplication Law.
A.L. = Addition Law.

(a) The probability of a red ball being chosen is 5/9
$Pr(R_1) = 5/9$ $Pr(R_2) = 5/9$
$\therefore Pr(R_1 R_2) = 5/9 \times 5/9 = 25/81$. (M.L.)
Why does the multiplication law apply?
$\therefore$ The probability of two red balls being chosen is 25/81.

(b) $Pr(R_1) = 5/9$ $Pr(B_2) = 4/9$
$\therefore Pr(R_1.B_2) = 5/9 \times 4/9 = 20/81$ (M.L.)
$\therefore$ The probability of the first ball being red and the second black is 20/81.

(c) $Pr(B_1.R_2) = 4/9 \times 5/9 = 20/81$ (M.L.)
$\therefore$ The probability of the first ball being black and the second red is 20/81.

(d) Only one red ball being drawn can happen in two ways which are exclusive.
These are $R_1 B_2$ or $B_1 R_2$.
$\therefore Pr(1$ red ball only$) = 20/81 + 20/81 = 40/81$ (A.L.)
What is the probability that the man gets at least one red ball?

Example 2
John and Peter are equally good at chess. They play three games against each other. What is the probability that (a) John wins all three games, (b) he wins only the first two games, (c) he only wins one game?
Let W_1 = John wins first game, etc. L_1 = John loses first game, etc.

(a) Since John and Peter are equally good, the probability of John winning a game is 1/2.
$Pr(W_1) = \frac{1}{2} : Pr(W_2) = \frac{1}{2} : Pr(W_3) = \frac{1}{2}$.
$\therefore Pr(W_1.W_2.W_3) = 1/8$ (M.L.)

(b) $Pr(W_1.W_2.L_3) = \frac{1}{2} \times \frac{1}{2} \times \frac{1}{2} = 1/8$ (M.L.)

(c) John could win only one game in three ways,
$W_1.L_2.L_3.$ OR $L_1.W_2.L_3$ OR $L_1.L_2.W_3$.
Each way has a probability of 1/8.
$\therefore$ Total probability $= 1/8 + 1/8 + 1/8 = 3/8$ (A.L.)
The probability of John winning only one game is 3/8.

You could work out John's possibilities of winning **(W)** and losing **(L)** in the form of a **PROBABILITY TREE** such as the one shown opposite. Possible wins are shown in black and possible losses in red.

If you trace the paths through the branches you will see that the chances of winning the first game is $\frac{1}{2}$. When it is won the chances of winning

An alternative solution to Example 2: **The Probability Tree**

THE PROBABILITY SCALE

3rd GAME

2nd GAME

1st GAME

$\frac{1}{2}$ W

$\frac{1}{2}$ W $\frac{1}{2}$ L

$\frac{1}{2}$ W $\frac{1}{2}$ W $\frac{1}{2}$ L

$\frac{1}{2}$ $\frac{1}{2}$ L $\frac{1}{2}$ L

$\frac{1}{2}$ W $\frac{1}{2}$ W $\frac{1}{2}$ L

$\frac{1}{2}$ L $\frac{1}{2}$ W $\frac{1}{2}$ L

The parts of the probability tree which give the answers to Example 2.

(a)

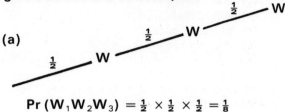

$$\text{Pr } (W_1 W_2 W_3) = \tfrac{1}{2} \times \tfrac{1}{2} \times \tfrac{1}{2} = \tfrac{1}{8}$$

(b)

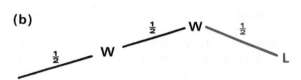

$$\text{Pr } (W_1 W_2 L_3) = \tfrac{1}{2} \times \tfrac{1}{2} \times \tfrac{1}{2} = \tfrac{1}{8}$$

(c)

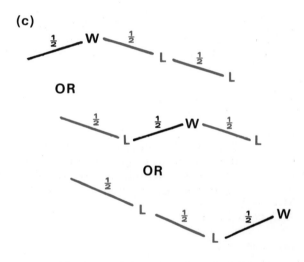

OR

OR

$$\text{Pr (1 win only)} = \tfrac{1}{8} + \tfrac{1}{8} + \tfrac{1}{8} = \tfrac{3}{8}$$

the second game is $\frac{1}{2}$ and in this problem the chance of losing it is also $\frac{1}{2}$. Trace the path for losing the first game and winning the next two.

To find the probability for any path through the branches one simply multiplies the probabilities shown in each branch which makes up the path. The probability tree is the multiplication law in the form of a diagram.

In Example 2(a) you were asked to find the probability of John winning three games. This path is shown in the diagram (a) above. Each

branch in the path has a probability of $\frac{1}{2}$. The probability for the whole path is therefore $\frac{1}{2} \times \frac{1}{2} \times \frac{1}{2} = 1/8$. So the probability of John winning all three games is 1/8. The solutions to the other parts of Example 2 are also shown in the diagram.

Use the probability tree to find the probability of (d) John winning only two matches, (e) John winning at least one match.

51

1. A not-so-smart electrician carries all his bulbs in one bag. He has 8 dud bulbs and 4 live ones. If he picks any three bulbs from his bag what is the probability he picks
   (a)   3 live ones
   (b)   only 2 duds
   (c)   at least 2 duds
   (d)   only the second one a dud?
   Hint: Draw a probability tree for this problem.

2. Mary is twice as good as Ann at tennis. They play four sets. What is the probability of
   (a)   Mary winning all the sets
   (b)   Mary only losing one set
   (c)   Mary and Ann getting two sets each?
   What is the most likely number of sets Mary will win?

3. An anti-aircraft rocket base has successfully shot down 750 out of 1000 aircraft which flew over it. What is the probability that (a) one aircraft will get past the rocket base, (b) that three out of three aircraft will get past the base, (c) that any one of three aircraft will get past the base. (d) If it is important that at least one aircraft should get past the base, is it better to send only one aircraft, two aircraft, three aircraft?

4. An insurance company estimates that the probability of any sports car driver having one accident in one year is $\frac{1}{10}$th. The average cost of such accidents to the insurance company is £750. (This includes payment for repairs, legal fees, clerical work and a small profit.)
   What should the insurance company charge for its sports car drivers' insurance policies.

For over 150 years the laws of probability were only used to analyse the outcomes of games. From these early beginnings grew the *THEORY OF GAMES* which is now used to analyse not only games and competitions but big business enterprises and even wars.

Examples III—Probability problems

1. A solid regular tetrahedron has four faces marked 1, 3, 5, 7. When it is thrown each number is equally likely to turn up. It is thrown twice.

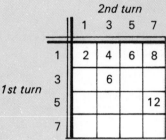

(a) Complete the table showing possible total scores for each pair of throws.
(b) What is the chance of the total being 4?
(c) What is the chance of the total being 8?
(d) What is the chance that the score will not be 14?
(e) What is the chance that the score will be greater than 8?

2. Draw up a table showing the possible scores when 2 dice are thrown.
What are the probabilities of:
(a) A score of 2
(b) A score of 5
(c) A score of 12
(d) A score of 13?
Which scores are most likely to occur and what is the probability? If the probability of a score, S, is taken as P (probability), draw a graph of P against S.

3. (a) A card is drawn at random from a full pack of 52 cards. What is the probability that the card will be:
   (i) an ace
   (ii) a red ace?
   (b) If two coins are tossed simultaneously, what is the probability that:
   (i) two heads will turn up at the first throw
   (ii) two heads will turn up on each of three consecutive throws?

4. There are 3 first division clubs, 4 second division clubs and 1 fourth division club left in the F.A. cup. Calculate:
   (a) the probability that a first division club will be drawn out of the hat first.
   (b) the probability that the first two out of the hat will be a first division club at home to a second division club
   (c) the probability that the first two out of the hat will be a first division club at home to either a second division club or the fourth division club.

5. (a) Distinguish between theoretical and practical probability.
   (b) What is the probability of throwing a total of 16 with 3 dice?
   (c) There are three routes from A to B. Mr. Brown sets off from A and Mr. Hobbs from B. If they reach the opposite ends without meeting, they each set off again. If neither of them take the same route twice, what is the probability that they meet on the first walk?

6. A carton of 12 pens contains three faulty pens. One pen is drawn from the carton. What is the probability that the pen is faulty? If the pen is not faulty, and it is not replaced what is the probability that on drawing a second pen from the rest it will not be faulty?

7. A box contains three white and two black counters. What is the probability that when a counter is drawn it is one of the white ones? If the counter is white and is not replaced, what is the probability that the next counter drawn is a white one also?

8. (a) If the probability that it will rain tomorrow is 0·35, what is the probability that it will not rain tomorrow?
   (b) The probability of a car driver having an accident, however small, in any year is 0·14. Out of 250 car drivers, how many may expect to have an accident this year?

9. If a number is selected at random from each of the sets 1, 2, 3 and 3, 4, 5, what is the probability that
   (i) the sum of the two numbers will be greater than 5
   (ii) the product of the numbers will be greater than 5?

10. Of 80 pupils in a certain year, 20 are specializing in mathematics and 30 are members of the athletic club; 40 of the pupils neither specialize in mathematics nor are members of the athletic club. Show these facts in a Venn diagram. If a pupil is selected at random, what is the probability that he:
    (i) both specializes in mathematics and is a member of the athletic club
    (ii) specializes in mathematics and is not a member of the athletic club?

11. Out of 10 rare books, 5 of which are especially valuable, 3 are taken at random by a thief. What is the probability:
    (a) that none of the 5 is included
    (b) that 2 of the 5 are included?
    Hint: Use probability tree.

12. A coin and a dice are tossed. Make an array of ordered pairs of all possible results. Find the probability of:
    (i) a head showing along with an odd number
    (ii) a head showing along with a prime number.

13. A chocolate box contains 20 chocolates, 6 of them have hard centres. What is the probability of getting:
    (i) 1 hard centred chocolate
    (ii) 1 soft centred chocolate
    (iii) not getting a hard centred chocolate on the first try?

14. 5 boys were in a race, all with approximately the same chance of winning. (i) What is the probability of any particular one of them winning? (ii) What is the probability of any particular one of them losing? (iii) If you were a bookmaker, what odds would you take on any particular one winning?

Revision exercises

Weighted averages

1. A sweet shop proprietor mixes 2 kg of sweets costing £1.80 per kilogram, with 4 kg of sweets costing £3.60 per kilogram. What is the cost per kilogram of the mixture?

2. In a grocer's shop, a man mixes 5 kg of coffee, at £3.85 per kilogram, with 1 kg of chicory at £1.25 per kilogram. At what price per kilogram (to the nearest p) must he sell it in order to make 50 per cent profit?

Visual statistics

3.

Age (years)	14+	15+	16+	17+	18+	19+
Pedestrians	7	6	15	11	7	9
Cyclists	24	31	25	13	8	15
All passengers	2	19	25	48	51	52
Drivers	0	0	1	1	8	20
Motor cyclists	1	0	50	87	88	111

The above table gives the deaths of teenagers in road accidents. Draw line graphs to show these figures.
What is the most dangerous age for (i) cyclists, (ii) passengers, (iii) motor cyclists?
Why is there zero for drivers aged 14 and 15?
What was the total number of 14–19 year olds killed on the roads?
What percentage of these were motor cyclists?
What item in the table is unusual?

4.

Diameter (cm)	·985	·990	·995	1·000	1·005	1·010	1·015
Frequency	2	10	50	75	10	2	1

The above figures gives the diameters of ball-bearings made by a machine. Draw a histogram of the data. What percentage of ball-bearings are between 0·995–1·005 centimetres? What is the mean diameter of the ball-bearings? What is the probability that the machine will produce a ball-bearing (i) greater than 1 centimetre diameter, (ii) less than 1 centimetre diameter? Estimate how many ball-bearings the machine will produce of diameter greater than the mean.

Probability

5. If a football match is assumed to have equally likely a home win, away win or draw, what is the probability
   (a) Of a draw?
   (b) List the possibilities for 2, 3, football matches. What are the possibilities that the results will be 2 draws, 3 draws respectively?
   (c) What is the probability of getting 8 draws from 8 matches?

6. Do a survey of the number of boys and girls in
   (a) families of one child
   (b) families of two children
   (c) families of three children.
   Work out the practical probabilities from your survey of
   (i) a family of three children containing only boys
   (ii) a family of two children containing only girls
   (iii) the families of one child containing only girls
   Compare your figures with the theoretical probabilities.

22 Horse racing, Bingo and Fruit machines

GAMBLING ON HORSES

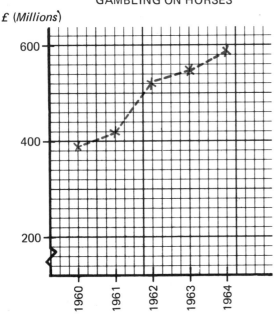

£ (Millions)

Lester Piggott riding *'Every Blessing',* **the winner of the Princess Elizabeth stakes at Epsom 1966.**
Over £600,000,000 was gambled on horses in 1965. This is more than enough to feed all the starving children in the world for the next five years.

More and more people are taking up gambling as a pastime. This includes horse racing and Bingo. All gambling is based on probabilities. The probabilities are always weighted in favour of the bookmaker. In other words the bookmaker makes a profit on most races.

Odds against and Odds on

If you back a horse at odds of 6–1 against, the chances are that it will lose. 6–1 against means the bookmaker reckons the horse has six chances of losing for every one chance of winning. He will pay the backer six times the amount he betted plus his original stake if the horse wins. If the horse loses, the bookmaker keeps the backer's stake. The probability of the horse winning at

6–1 is 1/7. Remember the probability of the horse winning is the one possibility of winning divided by the total possibilities (6 losses + 1 win).

What do you think odds of '2–1 on' means?
What are these odds in probability terms?
What fraction of your stake would the bookmaker pay if your horse won?

Bookmakers calculate the odds for a horse on its past performance and on the number of people backing it. If a lot of people back the horse, they cover themselves by shortening the odds **(What does this mean?)** and placing their own bet on the horse with a bigger bookmaker. If several bets of this kind are placed with the biggest bookmakers the odds on the horse are shortened even more. In this way the bookmaker insures himself against losses. If the heavily backed horse wins, he wins a little; if it loses, he makes a big profit.

Bingo

Bingo in the past few years has become a big business. Over 13,000 Bingo clubs have been formed and prizes of up to £5,000 are offered in the big clubs which are linked together by a telephone system (Telex).

Playing Bingo is easy. As you enter the Bingo Hall you are given a card which has 15 numbers on it. The steward blows a whistle to signal the beginning of a game and the caller draws numbered balls from a drum and calls the numbers out. If the number called is on your Bingo card, you put a ring round it. The first person to ring the 15 numbers on his card wins. He shouts 'House' or 'Bingo', the steward blows his whistle, the card is checked and the winner gets his prize.

The numbered balls go from 0 to 99 and each has an equal chance of being drawn. So the probability of any one number being drawn is 1/100.

What is the probability of the first three numbers called being on a person's card?

Some people think it is better to go to bigger Bingo clubs than smaller ones. They say the prizes are bigger and you have a better chance of winning a lot of money. The prizes certainly are bigger but since there are more people playing the probability of winning is less. If you are one of a hundred people playing Bingo then you have a probability of 1/100 of winning. If you are one of a hundred thousand playing in a Telex game your probability of winning is only 1/100,000. This is about 5,000 times less than the probability of a car being stolen in Central London! Yet most people would rather pay half-a-crown to join a game with a prize of £5,000 and a probability of only 0·000001 of winning than pay a shilling to play in a game where the prize is £5 and the probability of winning is 0·01. Many Bingo players recognise that they are losing money but are spurred on by the thought 'Somebody's got to win. Next time it might be me'. It might. But in the big games the chances are 0·99999 it might not!

Some of the estimated 14,384,000 regular Bingo players.

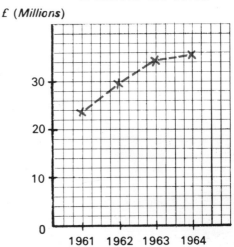

SPENDING ON BINGO

£ (Millions)

1961 1962 1963 1964

A BINGO CARD

Fruit Machines

Fruit machines have become a popular way of losing money. You put a coin in the fruit machine and pull a lever. This makes three drums in the machine revolve quickly, then they slow down and finally stop. Each drum has pictures of different fruits on it and if these fruits appear in a certain order when the drum stops you get a prize. Often the prize is just a few coins. Very occasionally a winning set of fruits turns up which gives you all the coins in the prize section of the machine. This is the 'jackpot'.

Fruit machines are designed so that the winning sets of fruit occur at irregular (chance) intervals. They pay out only a fraction of the money put into them. Often the machines are set to pay out only 10% of the takings. The rest of the takings go to the owners of the machine.

The theory of the fruit machine

This is how probability theory applies to the fruit machine.

The probability of getting a lemon on drum 1 is 1/8. The probabilities of getting lemons on drums 2 and 3 are also 1/8. Using the multiplication law the probability of getting three lemons is $1/8 \times 1/8 \times 1/8 = 1/512$. So this machine will give a jackpot prize only once in 512 times.

The probability of a pear on drum 1 is 1/8.
The probability of an orange on drum 2 is 2/8.
The probability of an orange on drum 3 is 1/8.
So the probability of winning 30 coins is $1/8 \times 2/8 \times 1/8 = 2/512$.
This prize will be paid only twice in 512 times.

Calculate the probabilities of winning the other prizes.

What is the probability of not getting a prize on any one try?

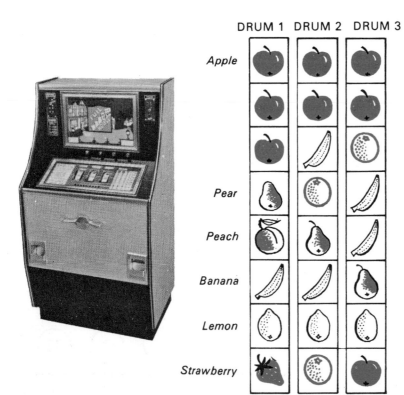

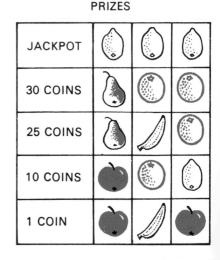

1. There are 12 horses in one race and 10 horses in another. If all the horses have an equal chance of winning, what is the probability that
   (a) a man who backs 4 horses in the first race backs the winner
   (b) a man who backs 1 horse in each race gets (i) both winners, (ii) the winner of the first race and a loser in the second, (iii) only the winner of the second race, (iv) only one winner, (v) no winners?

2. A man said that if a jockey wins twenty races in a row he would never back him in the twenty-first race because on the laws of chance he is bound to lose. Was the man right?

3. Change the odds for each horse into probabilities in decimal form.
   Find the total probability.
   How do bookmakers try to guarantee a profit?

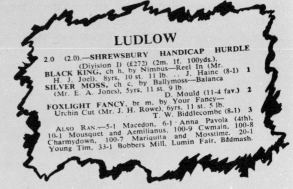

LUDLOW

2.0 (2.0).—SHREWSBURY HANDICAP HURDLE
(Division I) (£272) (2m. 1f. 100yds.).
BLACK KING, ch h, by Nimbus—Reel In (Mr.
H. J. Joel), 8yrs, 10 st. 11 lb. .. J. Haine (8-1) **1**
SILVER MOSS, ch c, by Ballymoss—Balanca
(Mr. E. A. Jones), 5yrs, 11 st. 9 lb.
D. Mould (11-4 fav.) **2**
FOXLIGHT FANCY, br m, by Your Fancy—
Urchin Cut (Mr. J. H. Rowe), 6yrs, 11 st. 5 lb.
T. W. Biddlecombe (8-1) **3**

ALSO RAN.—5-1 Macedon, 6-1 Anna Pavola (4th),
10-1 Mousquet and Aemilianus, 100-9 Cwmain, 100-8
Charmydown, 100-7 Mariquita and Mosstime, 20-1
Young Tim, 33-1 Bobbers Mill, Lumin Fair, Badmash.

4. A hundred thousand people are playing in a Telex Bingo game. What is the probability of the same person winning the first three games (a) if he has only one card in each game, (b) if he has two cards in each game?

5. In a similar game a Liverpudlian claimed he could mark 24 cards at once.
   What is the probability that in two games he will (a) win both, (b) win only one game, (c) win no games?
   Give your answers to four significant figures.

6. If there are only 80,000 different cards and only two cards of each sort, what are the chances of two people getting identical cards?

Every time the chimpanzee on the left puts a token in the machine (called a Chimpomat) he gets a peanut. Every time the man on the right puts a coin in the fruit machine he probably loses it.

23 Binomial probability

If you get married and have two children you could have two boys, or a boy and a girl, or a girl and a boy, or two girls. You can work out the probabilities using a probability tree.

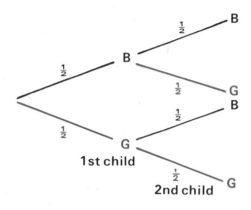

1st child

2nd child

OR   OR

You can see from the tree that you have twice as many chances of having a boy and a girl (in any order) as you have of having two boys or two girls. If we let BG = a boy and a girl (in any order) we can write the probabilities in this way

$\Pr(B,B) = \frac{1}{4}$ $\Pr(B,G) = \frac{1}{2}$ $\Pr(G,G) = \frac{1}{4}$

What percentage of families of two children do you expect to have a boy and a girl?

You can use the probability tree to work out the probabilities of having 0, 1, 2 or 3 girls in a

family of three children. The results are given in the relative frequency histogram shown below.

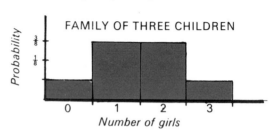

FAMILY OF THREE CHILDREN

What is the most likely number of girls in a family of three?
What is the mean number of girls you would expect to find in a large number of families of three?
What is the total area of the histogram?

Since relative frequency is the same as probability the histogram above may be called a **probability histogram.** Similarly, relative frequency distributions are called **probability distributions.**

Binomial probability

You can use simple algebra, instead of the probability tree, to work out the probabilities. This was an idea worked out by Sir Isaac Newton. Let us look at the way he would have worked out the probabilities for two children.

Let B = probability of having a boy.
    G = probability of having a girl.
$B = \frac{1}{2}$ and $G = 1 - \frac{1}{2} = \frac{1}{2}$
For two children we would have written $(B + G)^2$ and expanded it
$$(B + G)^2 = B^2 + 2B.G + G^2$$
$$= B.B + 2B.G + G.G$$
$$= \tfrac{1}{2}.\tfrac{1}{2} + 2.\tfrac{1}{2}.\tfrac{1}{2} + \tfrac{1}{2}.\tfrac{1}{2}$$
$$= \tfrac{1}{4} + \tfrac{1}{2} + \tfrac{1}{4}$$
(This gives a total of 1)
These are the same probabilities we got from the probability tree.
Now try to work out the probabilities for families of three children using Newton's method.

The expressions $(B + G)^2$ and $(B + G)^3$ are called **BINOMIAL GENERATING DISTRIBU-TIONS** (which is quite a mouthful!) They are called generating distributions because they generate or make the probability distributions. 'Binomial' means two parts such as, for example, heads or tails; wins or losses; successes or failures. A mathematician named Bernouilli proved that the binomial generating distributions always give the correct theoretical probability distributions. The proof is difficult to understand unless you know a lot of algebra.

Pascal's Triangle

Newton was in fact developing an idea worked out by Pascal who wrote out the triangular array of numbers shown opposite. The array can be carried on endlessly.

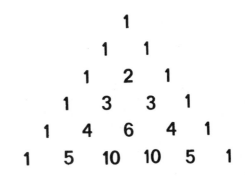

(a) How many numbers will there be in the 10th row?

(b) How do you get the numbers in one row from those in the previous row?
(*Hint*: Try adding in pairs).

(c) When you toss two coins the possibilities are
$$1\,HH + 2HT + 1TT$$
These numbers are in the third row of Pascal's triangle. The probabilities for two coins are $\frac{1}{4}, \frac{1}{2}, \frac{1}{4}$.
How do you get the 4 in the denominator from the third row of the triangle?

Pascal's triangle gives the coefficients of the generating distributions. It can be used to obtain the probability distributions for Pr. $= \frac{1}{2}$

1. Use a probability tree to expand $(F + S)^4$. F = failure and S = success. Compare the coefficients you obtain with the fifth row of Pascal's triangle.

2. Find the probability distribution for $(F + S)^4$ when $F = 0.25$.
   (*i*) What is the mean proportion of failures? What is the value of $4F$?
   (*ii*) Find the variance of the proportion of failures. (See Unit 12.) What is the value of $4FS$?
   (*iii*) What is a quick way of finding the mean, variance and standard deviation for a binomial distribution?

3. A boy does not know the answers to a YES-NO test of 16 questions so he answers 'yes' or 'no' at random. What is the probability that he will get 5 or more right?

4. A machine for putting tiny bags of salt into packets of crisps 'forgets' to do this about 1 in 10 times. Four packets of crisps were opened to see if they contained salt bags. Draw the probability histogram for the possibilities. What is the most likely number of packets without salt? If three packets had no salt what would you deduce about the machine?

24 Sampling

A gamekeeper asked a statistician to find out how many squirrels there were in a wood. The statistician caught 10 squirrels, marked their ears and let them go. Next day he caught another 10 squirrels and found that 2 of them had marks on their ears. The statistician then told the gamekeeper how many squirrels he thought were in the wood.

This is how he solved the problem.

Let P = the population of squirrels in the wood.

Then assuming the proportion of marked squirrels in the sample is the same as the proportion of the 10 marked squirrels to the whole population we have the equation

$$\frac{2}{10} = \frac{10}{P} \quad \therefore P = \frac{100}{2} = 50$$

So the statistician's guess (or estimate) of the number of squirrels in the wood was 50.

This estimate was based on only one sample. If the statistician was good at his job he would try to catch several samples of 10 squirrels from all over the wood. He would then draw a probability histogram of the number of samples taken which contained 0, 1, 2, 3 . . . marked squirrels. Here is a probability (relative frequency) histogram of the results.

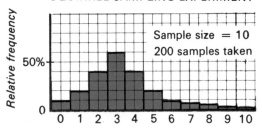

SQUIRREL SAMPLING EXPERIMENT

No. of marked squirrels in each sample

1. **What is the most likely proportion of marked squirrels in a sample?**
2. **What is the best estimate of the total population of squirrels?**
3. **What is the probability of getting a sample containing no marked squirrels?**

We used two important words in our description of the sampling experiment. They were *sample* and *population*.

A SAMPLE is a SELECTION from a population.

POPULATION means the WHOLE COLLECTION of people, animals or things the statistician is dealing with. It is the same as the universal set in Modern Mathematics.

We also told you in the squirrel experiment that a good statistician would take samples from all over the wood. He would do this to make sure he got areas where a lot of squirrels lived and areas where only a few squirrels lived. He would try very hard to arrange his sampling so that every squirrel in the wood had an equal chance of being caught. He would be trying to get what we call a **RANDOM SAMPLE.** This is a special form of unbiased sample.

Sampling and the theory of sampling is a very important part of statistics. We can find out a great deal about a population by studying random samples from it. In the squirrel experiment random samples were used to estimate the number of squirrels in the wood.

How do crows know which way to fly?

Canadian scientists have shown that migrating crows fly North when the days get longer and fly South when the days get shorter.

They took two samples of crows, marked their legs with different coloured rings for each sample and put them in different bird houses for the summer. One group had normal daylight and the experimental group had the light artificially controlled to correspond with the days of early spring. Both groups of birds were set free in autumn.

None of the normal group were reported North of the releasing point. A considerable number of the experimental group were reported North and very few were found South. By calculating the proportions of birds caught North and South the scientists were able to show that hours of daylight is an important factor in bird migration.

Sometimes people ask 'Why use samples?' The answer is that sometimes it is impossible to study the whole population directly, sometimes it would be too expensive to do so and sometimes it would take too much time.

Sampling is used in every branch of science and industry. For example, biologists and geologists analyse random samples of earth they collect from areas they are studying. Manufacturers examine samples of their goods to make sure they are of the right quality.

A classroom experiment

You can do an experiment in the classroom which is like the squirrel experiment. Put some unmarked counters in a bag. Do not count them. Add two marked counters to those in the bag. Take out four counters at a time and record the number of marked counters in the sample. Replace the counters and shake the bag. Repeat this a hundred times. Draw a probability histogram and then use it to estimate the total number of counters in the bag. Unlike the statistician in the squirrel experiment you can then check to see how close to the 'true' answer you were.

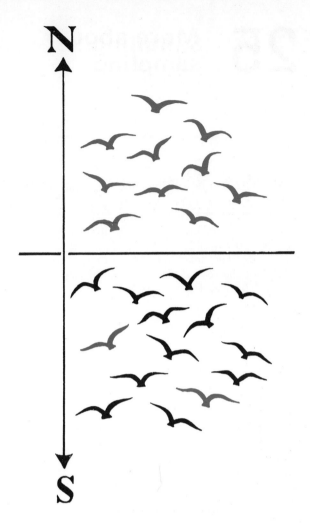

1. What do you understand by a 'random sample?'

2. Which of the following would you study by sampling? Give a reason for your answer.
    (*i*)   The length of life of cathode ray tubes.
    (*ii*) The number of people in the world.
    (*iii*) The safety cords on parachutes.
    (*iv*) The reasons given for absence by 4th form boys on the day of a Test Match.
    (*v*)   The 'Top Ten' discs of the week.

3. What might be wrong in taking these samples as typical of the population of England?
    (*i*) Londoners, (*ii*) people using London Airport, (*iii*) every tenth person listed in the telephone directory, (*iv*) people in restaurants, (*v*) teenagers, (*vi*) people whose names begin with the letters Ma . . .

25 More about sampling

Sampling in Industry

We have mentioned that one important use of sampling is to make sure that manufactured goods are of the right standard. For example, plastic toy makers employ sample inspectors to check the quality of the toys coming off their machines. The machines are sometimes set so that $\frac{2}{3}$ of the toys made are of good quality and $\frac{1}{3}$ are defective. The reason is shown in the diagram below.

PRODUCTION COSTS

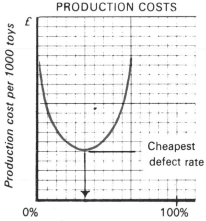

If the inspectors take random samples of 5 toys from a machine, they can decide if the machine is working at the correct defect rate. This is how they do it.

They find the number of defective toys in the sample of 5 taken from the machine and check this number against the sampling charts. If there are only 1 or 2 defectives in the sample they pass the whole batch of toys since according to the sampling chart the probability of getting a sample containing 1 or 2 defectives is 65·6% (32·8% + 32·8%). If the machine contains 3 defectives they take further samples. If the sample contains 4 or 5 defectives, they stop the machine and reset it. The sampling charts are based on 'Binomial Probability' calculations. The binomial generating distribution is $(\frac{2}{3} + \frac{1}{3})^5$.

SAMPLING CHART FOR TOYS

Defect rate $\frac{1}{3}$
Sample size 5

Defects in each sample

Defects	Pr.	%	Instructions
0	$\frac{32}{243}$	13·2	Pass whole batch
1	$\frac{80}{243}$	32·8	
2	$\frac{80}{243}$	32·8	
3	$\frac{40}{243}$	16·4	Watch this machine
4	$\frac{10}{243}$	4·1	Stop and Reset
5	$\frac{1}{243}$	0·41	
Total	1·0	99·71	

What is the probability that a sample will contain 4 or 5 defective toys?

In what per cent of samples would you expect to find no defective toys?

If 300 samples were taken, how many would you expect to find containing 5 defective toys?

Find the mean number of defective toys per sample.

Why is the total area of the probability histogram equal to 1?

Sampling in Advertising

Sometimes you see advertisements such as these. It is easy to get the result '9 out of 10 people prefer this. . . .'. All you do is keep on asking people until you get 9 out of a particular 10 giving you the answer you want. In other words, you use biased sampling and do not disclose it to your readers. Look at the statistics and claims of advertisements very carefully. You will often find some distorted statistics and biased sampling very cleverly disguised.

Sampling People's Opinions

Finding out what people think by taking a sample of their opinions is difficult to do properly. Sometimes the person being interviewed may be in a hurry, or in a bad mood, or not understand the question, or not want to answer it truthfully. Some of the dangers are shown in the cartoons. Try to work out what is wrong with the question in each cartoon. Is there anything else wrong with the interviews shown in the cartoons?

Nowadays great care is taken with the design of questionnaires and interviews. Even so you should always be a little suspicious of the reports of surveys you read in the newspapers. Whenever you read a report of a survey ask yourself, 'How did they find that out?'

Steel or plastic balls   **Sample of 10 balls**   **Sample of 20 balls**

A Sampling Experiment

You can use sampling bottles such as those shown above for experiments in the classroom or at home. Take a bottle which contains 40% black and 60% red balls (by weight). Adjust the glass tube so that you get a sample size of 5 balls. Record the number of black balls in the sample. Shake the bottle and take 50 samples recording the results in each case. Take several people's results, group them and draw a histogram showing the frequencies for 0, 1, 2, 3, 4 and 5 black balls. Convert the frequencies to probabilities. Try to find a way of *calculating* the probabilities and compare these with the results you got in your experiment and also with the total results.

1. Work out sampling charts for a machine with a defect rate of 50% for a sample of four items.
    (a) What is the probability of getting a sample containing no defectives, at least one defective, no more than three defectives?
    (b) How many defectives per sample would you accept before stopping the machine?
    (c) What is the mean and standard deviation of the number of defectives?

2. In a survey 720 housewives were asked which brand of detergent they used. The following replies were obtained:

Brand:	Bleak	White-it	Sparkle	Snowy	No particular choice
No. of housewives	230	124	68	186	112

Estimate how many housewives in a population of 14,400 use Bleak and Snowy.

The Quincunx or Binomial machine

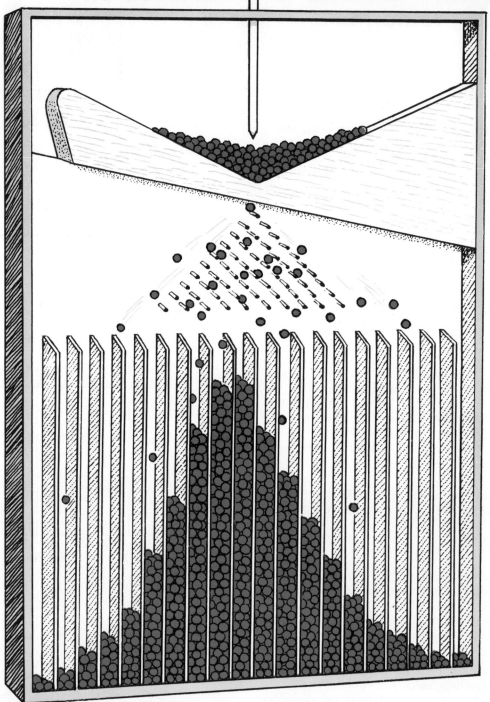

When the peg at the top is raised, the balls fall one at a time striking the pegs. As they collect in the channels, they build up a probability histogram. The machine, designed by Galton in the nineteenth century, is the forerunner of our modern pin-tables.

26 From binomial to normal

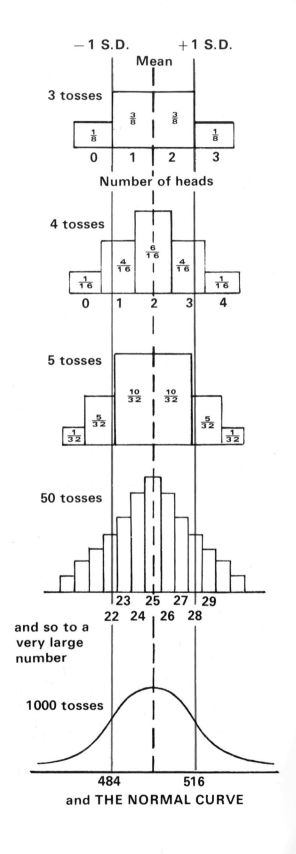

−1 S.D.   +1 S.D.
Mean

3 tosses

$\frac{3}{8}$ $\frac{3}{8}$

$\frac{1}{8}$ $\frac{1}{8}$

0 | 1 | 2 | 3

Number of heads

4 tosses

$\frac{6}{16}$

$\frac{4}{16}$ $\frac{4}{16}$

$\frac{1}{16}$ $\frac{1}{16}$

0 | 1 | 2 | 3 | 4

5 tosses

$\frac{10}{32}$ $\frac{10}{32}$

$\frac{5}{32}$ $\frac{5}{32}$

$\frac{1}{32}$ $\frac{1}{32}$

50 tosses

23 25 27 29
22 24 26 28

and so to a very large number

1000 tosses

484   516

and THE NORMAL CURVE

During the past few units you have often found the mean and standard deviation of a binomial distribution. Now that you understand what to do, we are giving you the formulae in statistical language. If $(P + Q)^n$ is a binomial generating distribution where P and Q are probabilities and n is the number in each sample then

The mean of the distribution $= n \times P$

The standard deviation $= \sqrt{n \times P \times Q}$

Follow the probability histograms down the page for tossing 3, 4, 5, 50 and 1,000 coins at a time. The probability histograms show you the results you would expect to get if you repeated 3, 4, 5, 50 and 1,000 tosses several times and recorded the number of heads you got on each try (or trial). The probabilities shown in the histograms have been calculated from the binomial distributions. You can see that the histograms grow closer and closer to the normal curve as you increase the number of coins being tossed.

The histograms are probability histograms and the normal curve shown is called **A NORMAL PROBABILITY CURVE** because it is a normal curve on a probability or relative frequency scale.

The black line on the histograms shows the mean number of heads you would expect to get. The red lines show the value of −1 standard deviations (S.D. for short) below the mean and +1 S.D. above the mean.

Write down the binomial generating distribution for each of the diagrams.
Work out the mean and the S.D. of the number of probable heads in each diagram.
What is the total area under each histogram? Under the normal curve?

The normal probability curve

You can see how a binomial distribution can grow into a normal distribution. You may also remember from Section 13 that the important property of the normal curve and its standard deviation is:

The mean ± 1 S.D. gives the middle 68·3% of the frequencies.
The mean ± 2 S.D. gives the middle 95·4% of the frequencies.
The mean ± 3 S.D. gives the middle 99·7% of the frequencies.

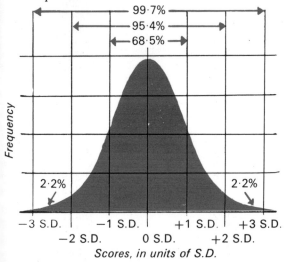

Scores, in units of S.D.

Since you can easily work out the mean and S.D. of a binomial distribution and you know the properties of the normal curve, you can use these facts together to solve problems on the binomial distribution when the sample size, n, is big. Usually we use the normal curve properties when n is greater than 50. This saves a lot of calculation and is accurate enough for most purposes. Below is an example for you to study:

1,000 pennies were tossed several times and the number of heads on each trial recorded. Work out the number of heads you would expect to get approximately on 68%, 95% and 99·8% of the trials. What conclusion would you draw about the penny if it came down heads 600 times out of 1,000 fair tosses?

The binomial distribution is $(H + T)^{1000} = (\frac{1}{2} + \frac{1}{2})^{1000}$
The mean number of heads is $1000 \times \frac{1}{2} = 500$
The S.D. of the number of heads is
$$\sqrt{1000 \times \tfrac{1}{2} \times \tfrac{1}{2}}$$
$= 15·81 \simeq 16$ for ease of working.
68% of the number of heads expected will be in the range Mean $\pm$ 1 S.D.
68% of the trials will probably contain between 484 and 516 heads.
Similarly 95% of the trials will probably contain between 468 and 532 heads.
Similarly 99·7% of the trials will probably contain between 452 and 548 heads.
Tossing one fair penny 1000 times is the same as having one sample of 1,000 fair pennies.
The probability of getting 600 heads with a fair penny is very small indeed. So we would conclude that the penny is almost certainly biased.

---

1. A Yes-No test contains 50 questions. Work out the mean and standard deviation of the number of answers which could be obtained by pure guess work. What is the probability of guessing more than 35 of the 50 questions correctly? Would 35 correct answers be a fair pass mark in this test?

2. 40% of the housewives in a city use a famous washing-up liquid. An interviewer said he had interviewed a random sample of 100 housewives and only 20 of his sample used the washing-up liquid. Is this result likely to be true?

3. A sample of 400 bolts was taken from a machine working at a defect rate of 10%. How many defective samples would you expect to contain between 28 and 52 defectives? If this machine was correctly set and you found 80 defectives in a sample of 200 bolts, what conclusion would you draw about the sample?

27 The normal probability table

Standard score	Probability
−3	0·001
−2·9	0·002
−2·8	0·003
−2·7	0·003
−2·6	0·005
−2·5	0·006
−2·4	0·008
−2·3	0·011
−2·2	0·014
−2·1	0·018
−2·0	0·023
−1·9	0·029
−1·8	0·036
−1·7	0·045
−1·6	0·055
−1·5	0·067
−1·4	0·081
−1·3	0·097
−1·2	0·115
−1·1	0·136
−1·0	0·159
−0·9	0·184
−0·8	0·212
−0·7	0·242
−0·6	0·274
−0·5	0·309
−0·4	0·345
−0·3	0·382
−0·2	0·421
−0·1	0·460
0	0·500
+0·1	0·540
+0·2	0·579
+0·3	0·618
+0·4	0·655
+0·5	0·691
+0·6	0·726
+0·7	0·758
+0·8	0·788
+0·9	0·816
+1·0	0·841
+1·1	0·864
+1·2	0·885
+1·3	0·903
+1·4	0·919
+1·5	0·933
+1·6	0·945
+1·7	0·955
+1·8	0·964
+1·9	0·971
+2·0	0·977
+2·1	0·982
+2·2	0·986
+2·3	0·989
+2·4	0·992
+2·5	0·994
+2·6	0·995
+2·7	0·997
+2·8	0·997
+2·9	0·998
+3·0	0·999

The normal probability curve is easy to use for simple calculations and this prompted statisticians to work out **NORMAL PROBABILITY TABLES** based on the normal probability curve with a mean of zero.

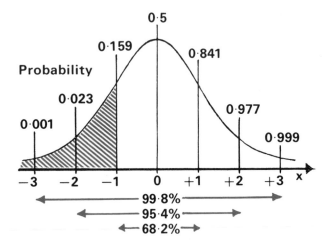

Probability or relative frequency is the area under the curve. The total area is 1. In theory the curve extends from minus infinity to plus infinity.
The probability levels shown for −3, −2, etc., are the areas under the curve from minus infinity to the standard score. The area from minus infinity to −1 S.D. (shown in red) is 0·159 or 15·9% of the total area under the curve.

The values along the x-axis are in standard deviations. The values are called Standard Scores (St.Sc. for short) and can be converted into probability levels. For example, in the diagram, the standard score of −1 S.D. gives the probability level of 0·159. In other words the probability of scoring this standard score *or less* is 0·159. Similarly the standard score of 0 gives a probability level of 0·5 so you would expect 50% of a normal population to get the mean standard score or less.

The normal probability table converts standard scores into probability levels. You will see from the table that a standard score of −1·5 S.D. gives you a probability level of 0·067. So if a person's standard score on a test was −1·5 S.D. it would mean that he was in the bottom 6·7% on this test. **What does a standard score of + 1 S.D. on a test mean?**

Converting to standard scores

A man scores 140 on an aircrew aptitude test. The mean score on the test is 100 and the standard deviation is 15. Only the top 0·5% are accepted. Is this man accepted?

The mean in standard scores is always 0.

Therefore the mean of 100 is the same as 0 S.D. in standard scores.

The man's mark of 140 is 40 from the mean.

Since the standard deviation is 15 this is equivalent to 40/15 = 2·7 (approx.) S.D. from the mean.

A standard score of 2·7 gives a probability level of 0·997 from the table. The man is in the top 0·3% and so is accepted.

In the example above we converted the ordinary score to a standard score in two stages.

First we subtracted the mean from the score, then we divided our answer by the standard deviation.

If we call the score x and the mean $\bar{x}$ and the standard deviation σ (pronounced sigma) we can put the instructions for these two stages in a formula:

$$\text{Standard Score} = \frac{x - \bar{x}}{\sigma}$$

For the previous example $x = 140$
$$\bar{x} = 100$$
$$\sigma = 15$$

$$\text{Standard score} = \frac{140 - 100}{15} = +2\cdot67 \text{ S.D.}$$

The probability level is then found from the table.

If the man had scored 138 marks would he have been accepted for aircrew?

Worked example. The average wage of workers in a factory is £4800. 3.6% of the workers earn £3000 or less. If the wages of the workers in the factory are approximately normally distributed what percentage of the workers earn more than £7200?

First we use the formula to find the standard deviation.

$$x = £3000 \quad \bar{x} = £4800$$

3.6% is the same as a probability of 0.036 which from the table is equivalent to a standard score of − 1.8

$$-1.8 = \frac{3000 - 4800}{\sigma} \quad \therefore \sigma = +\frac{1800}{1.8} = 1000$$

We then use the formula again to find the percentage of workers earning more than £7200.

$$x = £7200 \quad \bar{x} = £4800 \quad \sigma = 1000$$

$$\text{Standard score} = \frac{x - \bar{x}}{\sigma} = \frac{7200 - 4800}{1000} = 2.4$$

This gives a probability level from the table of 0.992. So the percentage of workers earning more than £7200 is 0.8%.

Remember you can only use the normal probability table when the figures you are using come from a normal distribution or nearly normal distribution.

1. Electric lamps have a mean life of 160 hours, with a standard deviation of 4 hours. Of a batch of 400 how many would you expect to have a life of (a) 150 hours or less, (b) between 150 and 162 hours? After how many hours would you expect 140 lamps to have failed?

2. A machine packs kilogram bags of sugar. The mean weight of the sugar in the bags is 1·03 kilograms and the standard deviation is 0·012 kilogram. Bags containing less than one kilogram are rejected. How many out of 50,000 would be rejected?

3. The distribution of marks in a C.S.E. examination was normal. 16% of the candidates got less than 40 marks and so failed. The mean mark was 50. Distinctions were awarded to candidates getting over 75 marks. 10,000 candidates took the examination. How many got distinctions?

28 Testing hypotheses

Levels of Significance

Mr. Brown tossed a penny in the air 3 times. It came down heads 3 times. He asked Mr. Hanson if the coin was biased. Mr Hanson said the penny was probably not biased, but it was difficult to say on only 3 tosses. So Mr. Brown tossed the penny 5 times and it came down heads 5 times. Mr Hanson thought for a moment and then said, 'The penny is probably biased.' Mr. Brown then tossed the penny 10 times and got 10 heads. Mr. Hanson said, 'The penny is almost certainly biased.' How was Mr. Hanson deciding whether the penny was biased?

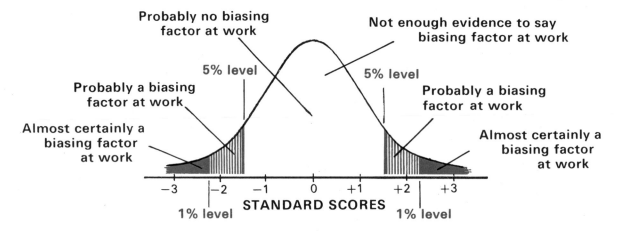

As a matter of fact he was using a simple idea chosen by statisticians, to help them make decisions. If the probabilities are in the top or bottom 5% of the normal curve, we say there is probably a biasing factor at work. If the probability is in the top or bottom 1% of the normal curve, we say there is almost certainly a biasing factor. The 5% and 1% levels are called **'LEVELS OF SIGNIFICANCE'**.

Statisticians chose the 5% level and 1% level as levels of significance or importance. If there is no biasing factor at work, you would only get a probability in the top 5% (or in the bottom 5%) of the curve 1 in 20 times. If there is no biasing factor at work, you would only get a probability in the top 1% (or bottom 1%) of the curve 1 in 100 times.

> 5% (0·05)—Significant—Probably biasing factor at work
> 1% (0·01)—Highly Significant—Almost certainly biasing factor at work

You can see in the second diagram how Mr. Hanson was deciding whether the penny was biased.

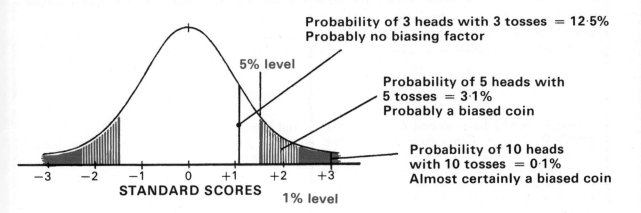

Probability of 3 heads with 3 tosses = 12.5%
Probably no biasing factor

Probability of 5 heads with 5 tosses = 3.1%
Probably a biased coin

Probability of 10 heads with 10 tosses = 0.1%
Almost certainly a biased coin

5% level

1% level

STANDARD SCORES

A penny was tossed 4 times and came down tails 4 times. Was the penny biased?

The Null Hypothesis and Experiments

We have described to you how Mr. Hanson used the levels of significance to help him decide whether the penny was biased. You may not have realised it, but Mr. Brown was really carrying out a simple experiment to find out whether the penny was biased.

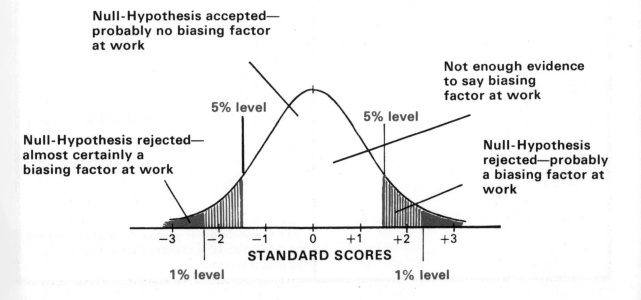

Null-Hypothesis accepted—probably no biasing factor at work

Not enough evidence to say biasing factor at work

5% level

5% level

Null-Hypothesis rejected—almost certainly a biasing factor at work

Null-Hypothesis rejected—probably a biasing factor at work

STANDARD SCORES

1% level

1% level

If he was doing the experiment seriously this is what he would have done:

1. First he would have written down his **Hypothesis.** Hypothesis is the correct word for the idea which is going to be tested.	*Hypothesis*: This penny is biased.

2. Next he would have written down his **Null Hypothesis.** This is always *basically* the same. 'There is *no* biasing factor at work.'
    We stick to the Null Hypothesis until we are sure there are biasing factors probably at work. (This is rather like the idea that a person is innocent until proved guilty.)
	Null Hypothesis:
	    This penny is a fair penny (until proved otherwise).

3. Then he would have done the experiment as carefully as he could, to make sure *he* does not introduce bias into the experiment. He would have written down the precautions and the results.	*Method and Precautions*:
	    A penny was tossed in the air 10 times. The penny was shaken in the hands first and each toss was at a different height. This was to try to avoid introducing bias.
	
	Results:
	    The penny came down heads 10 times in 10 tosses.

4. Then he would have calculated the probability of his result and compared this with the levels of significance.	*Calculation*:
	    Pr (10 heads in 10)
	        $= (\frac{1}{2})^{10} = 0\cdot001$
	        $= 0\cdot1\%$
	    This is beyond the 1% level and so is highly significant.

5. Then he would have stated his conclusion.	*Conclusion*: The probability of getting 10 **heads** is beyond the 1% level. It is therefore almost certain that the coin is biased.

More about testing hypotheses

You can use the normal probability table to decide whether the result of an experiment is significant.

Suppose a penny *tossed fairly* came down heads 15 times in 20 tosses. Is the penny biased?

Hypothesis: This penny is biased.
Null Hypothesis: This penny is a fair penny.
Calculation (based on Normal Probability Table)

You may remember $\dfrac{x-\bar{x}}{\sigma}$ gives the Standard score which gives the probability level. x in this experiment is 15, $\bar{x}$ is 10 heads since if the coin is a fair penny you would expect it to come down heads 10 times in 20. The standard deviation is $(\sqrt{npq}) = \sqrt{20 \times \frac{1}{2} \times \frac{1}{2}} = 2.236$.

So $\dfrac{x-\bar{x}}{\sigma} = \dfrac{15-10}{2.236} = 2.2(36)$ (Standard Score).

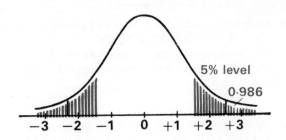

A Standard Score of 2·2 yields a probability of 0·986. This is in the extreme end of the normal curve. So the result is significant at the 5% level.

Conclusion:

The null hypothesis is rejected. The coin is almost certainly biased.

A simple experiment —see if you can introduce bias. Toss a penny 40 times. Try to get heads as many times as you can by tossing in a biased way. Collect the class results and work out the mean number of heads per 40 tosses for the class. Set out the experiment in your books. Find out whether: (*a*) Your results are significantly biased. (*b*) The class results are significantly biased.

Which is easiest to bias 'significantly?' A die or a penny? Do you think the 5% and 1% levels of significance are low enough for a class experiment using dice?

Testing hypotheses

In this unit we have introduced you to some of the most important ideas in Advanced Statistics. Sociologists, psychologists, geographers and biologists all use levels of significance and test hypotheses in the way we have shown you.

Here are some examples:

1. Sociologists have discovered that the firstborn children in families in this country do very much better in school work than their younger brothers and sisters. The differences are significant at the 5% level.

   Does this mean that all firstborn children do better than their brothers and sisters?

2. Psychologists have shown that people who are slightly anxious are better drivers, as a rule, than those who are not anxious. The difference is significant at the 5% level.

   Does this mean that the more anxious you are the better you will be at driving?

Examples IV—Probability and sampling problems

1. Four unbiassed coins are tossed simultaneously. Find the probability that:
   (*i*) all four come down 'heads'
   (*ii*) two and only two come down 'heads'
   (*iii*) two or more than two come down 'heads'.

2. Assuming the chances of a baby being a boy or being a girl to be equal, find:
   (*a*) the probability that a family of six children consists of three boys and three girls
   (*b*) the probability that a family of six children contains at least four girls.

3. I toss three pennies one after the other.
   (*a*) Write down the eight possible results which I might get.
   (*b*) If 80 children each toss 3 pennies, in how many of these trials would you expect the result to be 2 heads and 1 tail?
   (*c*) In a survey of 800 families with three children, assuming boys and girls equally likely, how many families would you expect to have more boys than girls?
   (*d*) In the survey of 800 families with three children, how many families would you expect to consist of two girls and one boy?
   (*e*) In another experiment, I interview families with four children. What fraction of the number of families would have two boys and two girls in them?

4. An investigation into public opinion on V.A.T. is to be made by:
   (*a*) interviewing people in the street
   (*b*) asking questions by telephone
   (*c*) sending a letter to every householder.
   Criticise briefly each method.

5. (*a*) How do public opinion polls set out to establish the views of the British public on politics?
   (*b*) Why do these polls make several surveys in the few weeks before a General Election? What do they mean by 'a swing in favour of the Conservative Party'?
   (*c*) In what ways is the information gathered tabulated in the daily press?

6. During the 1939–1945 war, 1 ship in 10 was sunk on average on the journey to the Baltic. What was the probability that only half the ships of a convoy of six arrived safely? What is the mean number of ships one would expect to arrive safely from a convoy of 20 ships?

7. A question paper contains six questions, the answers to which are either 'yes' or 'no'. Find the probability that a person who answers the questions at random will have at least four answers right.

8. If the average number of rejects of razor blades is 10%, what is the probability of 0, 1, 2, rejects in a sample of 5?

9. 10 per cent of the number of ballistic missiles fired are failures. What is the probability that in four firings there are:
   (*i*) 0 failures
   (*ii*) 1 failure
   (*iii*) 2 failures
   (*iv*) 3 failures
   (*v*) 4 failures
   Draw a histogram of the probabilities. What is the modal number of failures?

10. Over a number of years at a famous seaside resort, 10 days in September are wet. A man takes a week's holiday there. What is the probability that:
    (*i*) all the days of his holiday are wet
    (*ii*) all the days of his holiday are dry
    (*iii*) not all the days are wet?
    How would you find the probability that 3 of the days were wet?

11. The average height of a London policeman is 178 cm. S.D. $\simeq$ 2.5 cm. What is the probability of finding a policeman 183 cm or more tall? A policeman under 163 cm? What percentage of police would you expect to be between 173–183 cm and 175.5–180.5 cm? Use your Normal Probability table to find how many policemen there are who are under 174 cm if total force is $\simeq$ 10,000.

12. The mean I.Q. of a large number of children of age 14 was 100 and the standard deviation of the distribution was 16. Assuming that the distribution was exactly normal, find:
    (*i*) What percentage of the children had an I.Q. (*a*) under 70, (*b*) under 80, (*c*) over 110, (*d*) over 140.
    (*ii*) Between what limits the I.Q.s of the middle 34 % of the children lay.

13. In a test of 50 questions, where the subject is required to answer only 'Right' or 'Wrong' to each question, what is the probability:
    (*i*) of 30 or more correct answers
    (*ii*) 35 or more correct answers,
         if the subject is guessing?
    In both cases use the mean and standard deviation of the binomial probability and the normal distribution tables.

29   Line fitting

Some of you may have done physics experiments and plotted the results on graphs. Below are two graphs showing how the length of a rod of metal increases as it is heated.

GRAPHS OF CHANGE OF LENGTH OF ROD AS TEMPERATURE CHANGES

I. IN THEORY

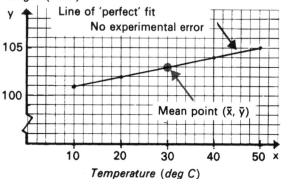

II. IN PRACTICE

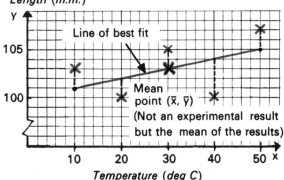

The red crosses show the actual results.
The black dotted lines show the amount of experimental error.

In theory the results should fit perfectly on to a straight line as they do in the top graph. Graph II shows the results you might get if you did the experiment.

In graph II the points are not in a straight line. This is because you can never do an experiment perfectly. There is always some error. The apparatus may not be perfect, the measuring instruments such as the thermometer, may not be perfectly accurate and you may not read the thermometer or do the measuring precisely. We call these errors 'experimental' errors.

In practice then you never get the points fitting exactly on to a straight line. Instead, we do the next best thing. We draw the straight line which goes as close to as many points as possible. This is shown in red in graph II.

The easiest way of finding the best straight line is to draw it. To help you find the best line of fit you can find the mean of the temperatures ($\bar{x}$) and the mean of the lengths of the rod ($\bar{y}$) and plot this point ($\bar{x}$, $\bar{y}$) on the graph. The best line of fit always goes through this point.

Regression

Line fitting is sometimes called **regression.** By drawing in the best line of fit you are moving the points on your graph back to where they would be if there was no experimental error. Regression comes from a Latin word *regressum*, which means to move back.

The correct name for the line of best fit in graph II is:

'The regression line of y upon x'; or 'The best estimate of y from x'. You can also have a line which is called 'the regression line of x upon y'. We will be saying more about this in the next unit.

Regression Equations

Regression lines are used in science and industry to find the best mathematical formula to describe an experiment or process. The formula based on a regression line is called a **regression equation.**

A simple way you can use to find the regression equation of a straight line is this:

1. Draw the straight line so that it goes as close to as many points as possible.

2. Find where this straight line cuts the 'y' axis. This is called the intercept, 'c'.

3. Find the gradient of the line. This is called 'm' and equals $\dfrac{\text{increase in } y}{\text{corresponding increase in } x}$

4. Substitute the values of c and m in the equation $y = mx + c$. This will give you the regression equation.
   'm' and 'c' are called the **regression coefficients** of the equation.
   '$y = mx + c$' is the general equation for any straight line.

   The diagram opposite shows you how to find the regression equation for the physics experiment. The equation is: $y = \frac{1}{10}x + 100$
   In physics you would write the equation
   $l_t = \frac{1}{10}t + 100$
   Try to put into words what the regression and physics equations mean.

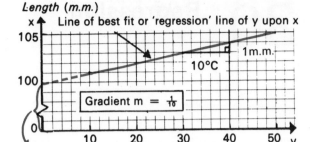

Length (m.m.)

Line of best fit or 'regression' line of y upon x

Gradient m = $\frac{1}{10}$

Intercept c = 100

Temperature (°C)

Regression equation is $y = \frac{1}{10}x + 100$

What is the length of the rod when the temperature is 0°C?

In this section we have shown you a simple way of finding the regression equation of a straight line of best fit. Sometimes the line of best fit is a curve. More complicated methods are needed to find the regression equation of a curve. You can find out more about regression equations of curves in a more advanced book such as Ractcliffe's *Elements of Mathematical Statistics*.

1. Work out the regression equations in the graphs shown below.

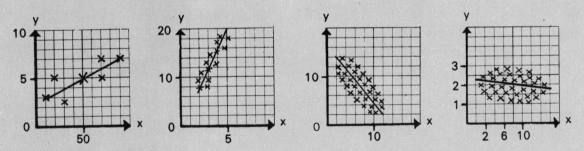

2. Below is a table showing you the daily temperature of some days in August and the amount of ice-cream sold on each day. Draw a graph of the data and fit the regression line of y upon x and find the regression equation. Use a scale of 1 cm = 2 gallons on the y axis and 1 cm = 2 degrees C on the x axis.

Temperature (x) (deg. C)	10	11	13·5	13·5	14	14	15·5	17	17·5	19
Ice-cream in gallons (y)	12	10	12	11	14	17	15	17	20	22

You may break the scale between 0°C and 10°C if you wish to. What is the best estimate of the amount of ice-cream he will sell on a day when the mean temperature is 22°C?

30 Regression

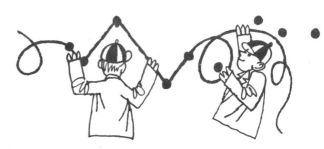

The diagrams below show you part of the results of a survey of heights and weights of schoolboys of the same age. The black line is '$y = mx + c$', the regression line of y upon x. You use this line to find the best estimate of the boys' weights from their heights. If you worked out the heights of each point above and below the regression line and added them together, you would find that the sum was approximately zero.

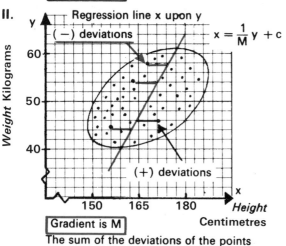

I.

Regression line y upon x

(+) deviations

$y = mx + c$

(−) deviations

Weight Kilograms

150   165   180   *Height Centimetres*

Gradient is m

II.

Regression line x upon y

(−) deviations

$x = \frac{1}{M} y + c$

(+) deviations

Weight Kilograms

150   165   180   *Height Centimetres*

Gradient is M

The sum of the deviations of the points from the regression line is zero or nearly so.

Mathematicians sometimes define the line of best fit as the one from which the sum of the positive and negative deviations is a minimum. You should be able to see why from the diagrams.

Diagram II shows the regression line of x upon y. You would use this line to find the best estimate of their heights from their weights.

Diagrams I and II are called **Scatter Diagrams**. These scatter diagrams show the scatter or distribution of heights and weights amongst a group of schoolboys. The scatter diagrams show you that:

The taller boys tend to be heavier.
(The regression line of y upon x)
The heavier boys tend to be taller.
(The regression line of x upon y)

The two statements describe in words the relationship between the heights and weights of the boys. The regression lines and the regression equations do the same thing in mathematical language.

Calculating regression equations

Drawing regression lines and finding the regression equations is easy to do. It is also easy to be wildly inaccurate! On the next page is a simple method of calculating the regression line directly from the data. The method is simple but the proof of it is complicated.

Example: Find the regression line of y upon x for the data given in the following table.

x	1	2	3	4	5
y	4	6	11	12	16

The equation of a straight line is $y = mx + c$.

We find the regression equation for the line of best fit by substituting the values of x and y in the equations $y = mx + c$ and $xy = x(mx + c)$. Then finding the *total* equations for $y = mx + c$ and $xy = x(mx + c)$ and solving them as simultaneous equations.

x	Substituting in $y = mx + c$	and in $xy = x(mx + c)$
1	$4 = 1m + c$	$1 \times 4 = 1(1m + c)$
2	$6 = 2m + c$	$2 \times 6 = 2(2m + c)$
3	$11 = 3m + c$	$3 \times 11 = 3(3m + c)$
4	$12 = 4m + c$	$4 \times 12 = 4(4m + c)$
5	$16 = 5m + c$	$5 \times 16 = 5(5m + c)$
	$49 = 15m + 5c \rightarrow \text{I}$	$177 = 55m + 15c \rightarrow \text{II}$

Solving the simultaneous equations I and II gives $m = 3$ and $c = \frac{4}{5}$

$\therefore$ The regression equation is $y = 3x + \frac{4}{5}$

Plot the points and the line to see how they 'fit'.

A STATISTICAL MODEL FOR THE CLASSROOM

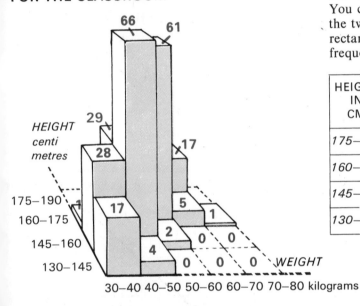

HEIGHT centimetres

175–190
160–175
145–160
130–145

30–40 40–50 50–60 60–70 70–80 kilograms

WEIGHT

Dimensional Histograms

You can show grouped data for two variables in a two-way table. The number in each class rectangle is a frequency. For example, nobody was between 175–190 cm tall and also weighed between 70–80 kg; 17 people were between 175–190 cm tall and weighed between 60–70 kg. You can construct a 3-dimensional histogram for the two-way chart. You build a box on each class rectangle. The height of the box represents the frequency.

HEIGHT IN CM	Class Rectangle			Frequency	
175–190	0	0	17	17	0
160–175	1	29	61	5	1
145–160	28	66	2	0	0
130–145	17	4	0	0	0
	30–40	40–50	50–60	60–70	70–80
	WEIGHT IN KILOGRAMS				

1. Find the sum of the deviations of the points above and below the regression line in Question 2 in Unit 29.
2. Find the sum of the deviations of the following set of figures from their mean:
   12,10,14,15,16,13,17,18,15,20.
3. What is the connection between the regression line of a set of points and the mean of a set of figures?
4. Find the regression line of y upon x for the following distribution:

x	0	1	2	3	4	5	6
y	16	13	9	6	4	1	0

5. Calculate the regression line of x upon y using the equation $x = My + c$, and $xy = y(My + c)$. (The method is the same as that of example 2 above.)
6. Draw the two regression lines on the same graph. What do you notice about the two regression lines?

31 Closeness of fit and correlation

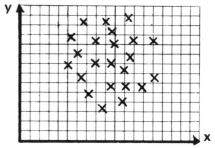

No regression line describes this data

Regression lines and regression equations are a shorthand way of describing the relationships between variables such as the heights and weights of a group of schoolboys or the increase in the sales of television sets and the decrease in cinema attendances.

The regression lines and equations which you get by drawing and calculation are the best shorthand descriptions that you can get of the relationship between the two variables. But, as you know, the 'best' can be far from perfect.

If the scatter diagram of the data is spread out over a large area, then the data does not fit closely to the regression line which is therefore a very poor description of the relationship between the two variables. If the points on the scatter diagram fit fairly closely to the regression line, then the line is a good description of the relationship between the variables. If the points of the scatter diagram fit *exactly* on to the regression line, then the line is a perfect description of the relationship between the two variables.

Statisticians have worked out several ways of measuring the closeness of fit of the data to the regression lines so that they can decide whether the lines and the regression equations are good descriptions of the relationship between the variables.

One easy way is this:

1. Draw in the regression lines of y upon x (shown in black) and x upon y (shown in colour) on the scatter diagram.
2. Measure the angle between the two regression lines and find its cosine.
3. If the cosine is fairly close to ± 1 then the data fits closely to the line. If the cosine is close to zero, then the data is widely scattered and so the regression line is a very poor description of the relationship between the variables.

The cosine of the angle between the regression lines is a measure of the closeness of fit of the data to the regression line.

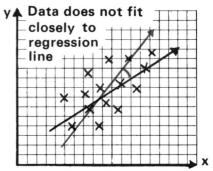

Therefore regression line a poor description

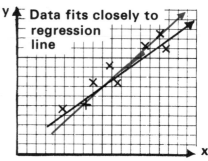

Therefore regression line a good description

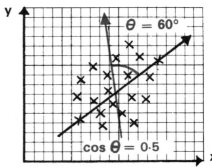

$$\theta = 60°$$
$$\cos \theta = 0.5$$

Data does not fit closely to regression line

We write this in the form of an equation

$$r = \cos\theta$$

where r is the measure of closeness of fit,

   θ is the angle between the two regression lines.

We have another name for the measure of closeness of fit. It is **CORRELATION.** r is called the **CORRELATION COEFFICIENT.** The correlation coefficient tells us whether the relationship between two variables is weak, good or perfect. You will be learning more about this in the next Unit.

Calculation of the correlation coefficient

You can calculate r, the correlation coefficient, from the gradients of the two regression lines.

r is given by the equation $r = m/M$

m is the gradient from the regression equation $y = mx + c$

M is from the regression equation $x = \dfrac{1}{M}y + c$

TELSTAR was the first communications satellite to go into orbit. Mathematicians worked out the path that Telstar should take. Astronomers plotted the path which Telstar actually took. The statisticians obtained the best line of fit from the astronomer's observations and calculated the regression equation. The best line of fit was very close to the path worked out by the mathematicians. The regression equation was very similar to the formula they used.

Statisticians often help other scientists to decide whether their experimental results agree with their theories.

Incidentally, the equation worked out for Telstar's path was in three dimensions and so contained three variables. The regression equations you have been studying are for two dimensional paths and so contain only two variables, x and y.

The table gives the marks in Mathematics (x) and the marks in Physics (y) for four boys.

Construct a scatter diagram for the set of paired values.

Draw the regression line of y upon x and the regression line of x upon y indicating which is which. What is the coefficient of correlation between x and y?

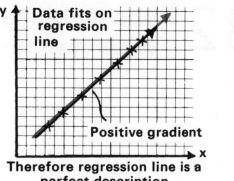

Data fits on regression line

Positive gradient

Therefore regression line is a perfect description

I

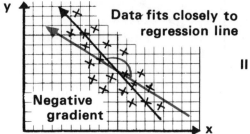

Data fits closely to regression line

Negative gradient

Therefore regression line is a good description

II

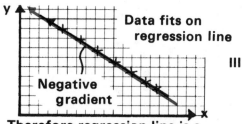

Data fits on regression line

Negative gradient

Therefore regression line is a perfect description

III

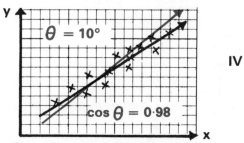

$\theta = 10°$

$\cos\theta = 0.98$

Therefore data fits closely to regression line

IV

Mathematics (x)	30	50	60	60
Physics (y)	30	40	40	50

32 Correlation and explanation

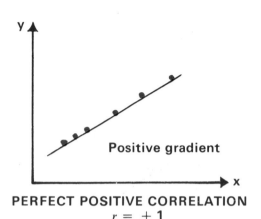

PERFECT POSITIVE CORRELATION
$r = +1$

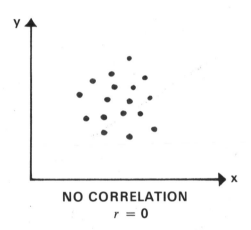

NO CORRELATION
$r = 0$

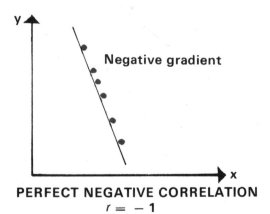

PERFECT NEGATIVE CORRELATION
$r = -1$

The three diagrams show you three kinds of correlation. In the first y increases as x increases. The data fits perfectly on to the regression line which has a positive gradient. We call this a **PERFECT POSITIVE CORRELATION.** The value of the correlation coefficient $r = +1$. The second diagram shows a scatter diagram of two variables which do not have a regression line. We call this **ZERO CORRELATION.** In the third diagram the regression line has a negative gradient. As you move along the x-axis the values of y get less and less. We call this **PERFECT NEGATIVE or INVERSE CORRELATION.** The value of the correlation coefficient $r = -1$.

The diagrams on page 85 show you the three important points on the **CORRELATION SCALE.** The highest point on the scale is $+1$, which stands for perfect positive correlation. The middle point is 0 and the lowest point is -1, which stands for perfect negative correlation.

Correlations with coefficients between $+0.8$ and $+1$ or -0.8 and -1 are the important ones. Usually research workers look for explanations for these correlations. Correlations with coefficients between $+0.3$ and -0.3 are usually not considered important.

Correlation and Explanation

In the question on page 83 you found that there was a high positive correlation between the Physics marks and the Mathematics marks of a group of boys. You probably pointed out that to be good at Physics you need to be good at Mathematics. In this question you found a correlation and then looked for an explanation.

Whenever a scientist finds an important correlation he looks for an explanation of the correlation. The correlation itself does not explain anything. It only tells you that there *might* be a sensible explanation.

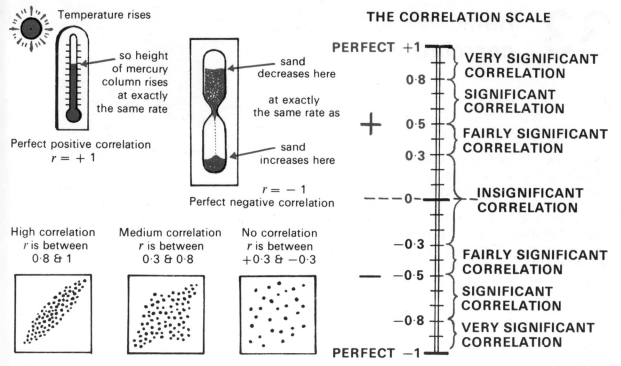

Temperature rises

so height of mercury column rises at exactly the same rate

Perfect positive correlation
$r = +1$

sand decreases here

at exactly the same rate as

sand increases here

$r = -1$
Perfect negative correlation

THE CORRELATION SCALE

PERFECT +1

0·8 — VERY SIGNIFICANT CORRELATION

SIGNIFICANT CORRELATION

0·5 — FAIRLY SIGNIFICANT CORRELATION

0·3

0 — INSIGNIFICANT CORRELATION

−0·3 — FAIRLY SIGNIFICANT CORRELATION

−0·5 — SIGNIFICANT CORRELATION

−0·8 — VERY SIGNIFICANT CORRELATION

PERFECT −1

High correlation
r is between
0·8 & 1

Medium correlation
r is between
0·3 & 0·8

No correlation
r is between
+0·3 & −0·3

For example, there is a high positive correlation between the number of storks nesting in Scandinavia and the increase in the number of births of babies there. Do you really believe that storks bring babies into the world? The explanation is that as the population increases more houses are built and so there are more places for storks to build their nests.

Not long ago someone measured the size of heads of a class of nine-year olds, gave them an intelligence test and worked out the correlation between the size of their heads and their intelligence. The correlation was highly positive. The obvious explanation was that the pupils with the biggest heads had the biggest brains and so were the most intelligent. The next week the same man measured the sizes of the children's feet and correlated these with their intelligence. Again the correlation was highly positive. The children with the biggest feet tended to be the most intelligent. Was this because they think with their feet? No! The sensible explanation is that the children with the biggest feet and the biggest heads tend to be the oldest in a class of nine-year olds and the oldest in the class *tend* to be the most intelligent.

Whenever you find a correlation you should ask yourself if there is a sensible explanation. Never accept a correlation on its face value.

Try to decide which of the following are positive or negative or close-to-zero correlations and whether there is a sensible explanation of the correlation. Give the sensible explanation if you can.
(a) The weight of pennies and their age.
(b) The cosine of an angle and its sine.
(c) The number of people attending a football match and the position of the team in the League Table.
(d) The rise in ice-cream sales and the increase in drownings in the sea during the summer months.
(e) The number of cigarettes smoked and the chances of getting lung cancer.
(f) Ability in art and ability at football.
(g) The road accident rate and the number of cars on the road.
(h) Absences from school lessons and success in the examinations.
(i) The increase in the sales of refrigerators and of central heating systems.
(j) The increase in Hire Purchase rates and the sales of cars.

33 Rank correlation

Some girls in a fifth form were arguing about whether girls who were good-looking were also good cooks. The teacher suggested to them that they should select 10 of the girls in the class to decide which were the best looking and the best cooks. They discussed the 10 girls' good looks and checked up on their cooking in domestic science lessons and produced this table of results:

Name of girl	Good looks Rank Order	Good Cooks Rank Order	Differences in ranks (d)	Differences squared (d^2)
Ann	2	1	+1	1
Brenda	7	10	−3	9
Deirdre	1	2	−1	1
Eva	6	3	+3	9
Georgia	9	6	+3	9
Harriet	4	5	−1	1
Ingrid	8	8	0	0
June	5	9	−4	16
Lorna	10	7	+3	9
Meryl	3	4	−1	1
			Total = 0 (Σd)	Total = 56 (Σd^2)

The girls then wanted to find the correlation between 'Good Looks' and 'Good Cooks'. One girl suggested that they should take the differences between the 2 rank orders and add them up. The answer was 0. As a matter of fact, the sum of the differences of ranks is always 0. Someone else suggested taking the total of the differences squared and using this.

Now it so happens that Professor Spearman invented a formula for measuring the correlation between ranks using the differences squared.

The formula is:

Rank Correlation coefficient $= 1 - \dfrac{6\Sigma d^2}{n(n^2-1)}$

n is the number of items being ranked.
Σd^2 is the Total of the differences between ranks squared.
(We use ρ (rho) for the rank correlation coefficient

to distinguish it from r, the ordinary correlation coefficient.)

Now if you use the rank correlation coefficient, ρ, the answer you get fits on to the correlation scale. A correlation of +1 means there is perfect agreement between the two sets of ranks, and a correlation of −1·0 means there is perfect disagreement between the two sets of ranks.

The girls correlated the ranks for good look and good cooks using the Spearman formula:

$$\rho = 1 - \frac{6\Sigma d^2}{n(n^2-1)}$$
$$n = 10, \Sigma d^2 = 56$$
$$\therefore \rho = 1 - \frac{6 \times 56}{10 \times (100-1)}$$
$$\rho = \frac{664}{990} = 0\cdot66 \text{ (to 2 significant figures)}$$

According to the correlation scale this is a significant correlation. In other words, in this group of fifth form girls, the girls who were good-looking *tended* to be good cooks, so the correlation between good looks and good cooking was high enough to be worth further investigation using a larger sample than ten.

Another use of rank correlation

You can use the rank correlation formula for measuring the correlation between 2 sets of marks. To do this you must first put the marks in rank order:

Example

Student	A	B	C	D	E	F
Chemistry	80	72	45	53	65	65
English	20	50	51	52	55	58
Chemistry (Rank)	1	2	6	5	3·5	3·5
English (Rank)	6	5	4	3	2	1
Differences in ranks (d)	−5	−3	+2	+2	+1·5	+2·5	$\Sigma d = 0$ (As a check)
d^2	25	9	—	—	—	—	$\Sigma d^2 =$

Complete the calculation. Is the correlation worth investigation? What is the disadvantage of using rank correlations on marks?

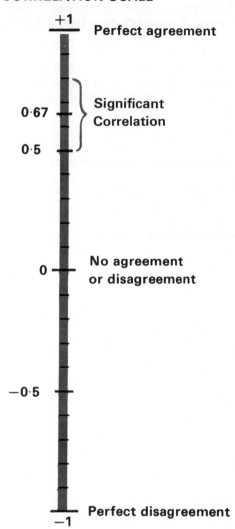

CORRELATION SCALE

+1 — Perfect agreement

0·67 — ⎫ **Significant Correlation** ⎭

0·5 —

0 — No agreement or disagreement

−0·5 —

−1 — Perfect disagreement

Spearman's formula

Some of you may want to know more about Professor Spearman's formula. If you calculate $\frac{d^2}{n(n^2-1)}$ for any sets of pairs of marks you always get an answer between $+\frac{1}{3}$ and 0. $+\frac{1}{3}$ is the maximum disagreement and 0 is the figure you get for no disagreement which is the same as perfect agreement.

So, $\frac{6 \times \Sigma d^2}{n(n^2-1)}$ always will give you an answer between $+2$ for maximum disagreement and 0 for perfect agreement.

So $1 - \frac{6\Sigma d^2}{n(n^2-1)}$ will always give you an answer between -1 for maximum disagreement and $+1$ for perfect agreement. So Spearman's formula fits the correlation scale.

1. A factory manager collected the following information on lateness of his workers.

	Arthur	Bert	Charlie	Derek	Eddy	Fred	George
Travelling Time Home to Work (mins.):	20	40	30	25	15	10	5
No. of times late in a month	16	1	2	5	0	12	17

    (a) Work out the rank correlation coefficient.
    (b) Is the correlation worth further investigation?
    (c) Why did the manager use 'Travelling time' rather than the distance 'Home to Work?'

2. Work out all the possible values of d^2 for 2 items and 3 items.
    (a) Can you get zero correlation with 2 items, with 3 items?
    (b) What is the most probable correlation you will get with 3 items?
    (c) Are rank correlations discrete or continuous?

Collected Examples

1. These diagrams are not clear and honest illustrations of statistics. Say what you think each diagram sets out to show and why it is misleading. Redraw them as you think they should be and label them appropriately.

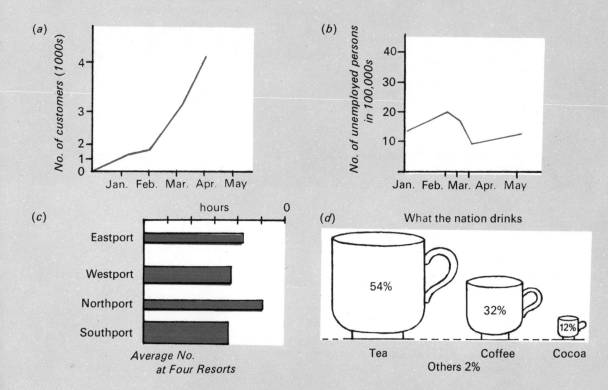

(a) No. of customers (1000s) — Jan. Feb. Mar. Apr. May

(b) No. of unemployed persons in 100,000s — Jan. Feb. Mar. Apr. May

(c) hours — Eastport, Westport, Northport, Southport
Average No. at Four Resorts

(d) What the nation drinks
Tea 54%   Coffee 32%   Cocoa 12%
Others 2%

2. Illustrate these two tables of statistical information in the most appropriate way.
   (a) The temperatures recorded on a thermometer throughout one day.

Time	6 a.m.	8 a.m.	10 a.m.	12 noon	2 p.m.	4 p.m.	6 p.m.	8 p.m.
Temperature °C	10	12	16	19	21	17	14	12

(b) The production of electricity in Western Europe in a certain year.
The figures represent 1,000,000's of units of electricity.

Method of production	Amount
Coal	341
Oil	34
Gas	103
Hydro-Electric	122

3. The following frequency table is of marks gained in an arithmetic examination by 100 pupils. The maximum possible mark was 100.

Marks	Frequency
1–10	2
11–20	3
21–30	3
31–40	7
41–50	15
51–60	22
61–70	18
71–80	15
81–90	10
91–100	5

(a) Construct a histogram to show the frequency distribution.
(b) What is the mode of the distribution?
(c) Assuming that the examination and the marking were without bias, what can you say about the way in which the marks are distributed?

4. (a) Use the frequency distribution in question 3 to draw up a cumulative frequency table of the marks. (Use intervals of 1–10, 1–20, 1–30, etc.)
(b) Draw a cumulative frequency diagram.
(c) Upon your diagram draw the cumulative frequency curve.
(d) From your curve estimate (i) the median,
(ii) the interquartile range of the marks.

5.

Fare per passenger	No. of tickets
5p	24
7p	34
9p	58
11p	79
13p	198
15p	240
17p	232
19p	102
21p	21
23p	12

The table shows the distribution of bus tickets bought by 1,000 people.
Find (a) The average fare paid per passenger
(b) The median fare
(c) The fare paid by the *modal group* of passengers.

6. The following percentage marks were obtained by a pupil in a certain examination: Maths 75, English 73, French 52, Physics 82, Geography 64, History 68.
(a) Find the arithmetic mean of these marks.
(b) If Mathematics and English are given treble weight and French and Physics double weight find the weighted mean of the marks.

7. A thousand tennis balls to be used at Wimbledon were tested by dropping from a height of 250 cm and measuring the height of the bounce. A ball is said to be 'fast' if it rises above 80 cm on the bounce and is not used. The mean height of bounce was 75 cm and the standard deviation was 1·9 cm.

(a) What percentage of balls were 'fast'?

(b) How many balls were fast?

(c) What was the probability of getting a fast ball in this sample of 1000?

8. (a) (i) If a true coin is tossed 5 times, what is the probability that it will come down tails every time?

    (ii) If the coin in (i) did come down tails 5 times in succession, what is the probability that it will come down tails in the next throw?

(b) Say why you think the following statements are right or wrong whichever the case may be.

    (i) If two coins are thrown up together there are three possible results—2 heads, 2 tails or a head and a tail— therefore the chance of a head and a tail is $\frac{1}{2}$.

    (ii) The death rate amongst head teachers is higher than amongst class teachers—therefore it is unwise for a teacher to seek promotion.

(c) For this question assume that in normal distribution all values beyond 3 standard deviations on either side of the mean can be ignored (see the diagram).

Copy the diagram and on one set of axes sketch the following:

    (i) A normal distribution with a mean of 100 and a standard deviation of 10.

    (ii) A normal distribution with the same population as in (i), a mean of 100 and a standard deviation of 5.

    (iii) Write down the range of each distribution and the interquartile range.

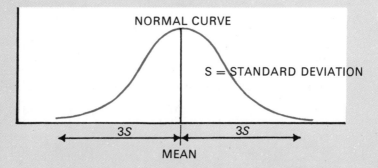

9. The data opposite represents the frequency distribution of marks in two examination papers, A and B. Copy the table in full and fill in the right-hand column.

Draw the cumulative frequency curves for both the examinations and answer the following questions:

(a) Calculate the median average for both examinations.

(b) Calculate the pass mark in A and B if in both 75% are successful.

Class	Frequency A	Frequency B	Cumulative Frequency	
11–15	7	3	7	3
16–20	14	14	21	17
21–25	38	22	59	39
26–30	45	37	104	76
31–35	52	49	156	125
35–40	52	60	208	185
41–45	53	67	261	252
46–50	55	61	316	313
51–55	58	70		
56–60	52	65		
61–65	47	46		
66–70	46	32		
71–75	38	23		
76–80	33	18		
81–85	21	11		
86–90	19	8		
91–95	14	9		
96–100	6	5		

10. Answer this question on the table below.

A sample of 4,400 adults (2,200 men, 2,200 women) are to be interviewed to find which programmes they watch on television. This sample has to represent the whole viewing population.

These assumptions are to be taken into account:

The age ranges of the population are in the following proportions: 15–19 : 20–29 : 30–49 : 50 years and over = 1 : 2 : 4 : 4.

The social groups are as follows:

Upper : Middle : Lower = 1 : 4 : 15.

Using this information complete the following table showing the composition of the sample.

| Age | Social Group | | | | | | Total | |
| | Upper | | Middle | | Lower | | | |
	Male	Female	Male	Female	Male	Female	Male	Female
15–19 years 20–29 years 30–49 years 50–over								
Totals								
	Total Upper	220	Total Middle	880	Total Lower	3300	Grand Total	4,400

Name one other factor which may have been taken into account in forming the sample.

11.

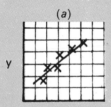
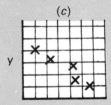

(a)   (b)   (c)

Diagrams (a), (b) and (c) are different scatter diagrams with 'the line of best fit' inserted where appropriate.

(i) Say what sort of information each diagram gives and in each case give an example of such a correlation in everyday life. What are the serious omissions in diagrams (a), (b) and (c)?

(ii) Three sets of information give the following coefficients of rank correlation (a) r = 0·85, (b) r = 0·13, (c) r = −0·87.

Explain the meaning of each of these coefficients.

12. The table below gives information on the length of T.V. programmes.

Length of programme (mins.)	Up to 30	30–45	45–60	60–75	75–105
Frequency	10	20	25	20	10

(a) Draw a line chart using the midvalues of the class intervals (length of programme) and the frequencies.

(b) What is the modal class of programmes?

(c) Are 50% of the programmes shorter than 45 minutes?

(d) What kind of visual chart would be best for showing the answer to (c)?

Answers and Notes

Unit 1 (*p.* 5)
1. Frequencies   (*i*) Cars 48
               (*ii*) Buses 5
               (*iii*) Total 94

Unit 2 (*p.* 7)
1. 7 and 8
3. Discrete: beer, pound notes, income of teachers, size of shoe, scores from two dice, colours of the rainbow,
Continuous: length of feet, colours of rainbow (colours may be considered as separate or merging into one another).
4.   (*i*) 800
    (*ii*) 3
    (*iii*) 3200 – 3999
    (*iv*) 41%
    (*v*) Some earn less than £3200

Unit 3 (*pp.* 8–9)
Answers to questions in the text
1. There were 55·5 million people in Great Britain.
4·0 million aged between 15 and 20.
2. 416,927.
21–24 for men; under 21 for women.
Yes.
3. This may have caught you out. It is not possible to estimate how many births from these figures unless you also know how many women there are in each age group.
30·91 babies per 1,000 women is the average (mean) number of babies born to every 1,000 women of that age group. It does *not*, of course, mean that each woman has ·03091 of a baby!
25–29 years is the most common age for women to have children.
4. 675·58 *thousands* died.
96,030 men died aged between 75 and 84.
Because there are fewer people to die.
One cannot say from this table since one needs to know how many men and women over the age of 85 are still living.
More women die over the 85 than men. This *may be* because there are more women alive in this age group of 85 and over.
5. A man earning £6,000 would probably spend £498 on clothes and £336 on fuel.
No. People and families have different spending habits. These figures are calculated from a large sample of different families living in different parts of Britain. The proportions are an average figure.

Answers to question in the exercise
3. Probably telephones and refrigerators since there are many people who have not bought these items yet.
No. A lot of people got married between 1965 and 1979, and some people have died.

Unit 6 (*p.* 15)
2. Under 16 figure must be at least 20, since under 14 is 20.
The table is either incomplete or wrong, since the last percentage given is 60%. The last percentage of a R.C.F.D. table should be 100%.
3. 13 hours or less
80%

Visual Statistics Problems (*pp.* 17–19)
1.   (*a*) 38
    (*b*) £16.80
    (*c*) 9/19
3.   (*b*) 72
    (*c*) 84
8.   (**a**) July
    (**b**) February
    (**c**) March, April, July, (October) January
9.   (**i**) Half-day closing
    (**ii**) 83
    (**iii**) 80%
10.   (**i**) £240
    (**ii**) Probably half-day closing
    (**iii**) Probably shop closes
    (**iv**) 33⅓%
    (**v**) No. Histograms use only frequencies

11.   (*i*) He was probably travelling in fairly heavy traffic in a town area.
    (*ii*) He probably stopped for a rest. Alternatively there was a hold-up on the road.
    (*iii*) He was probably on a motorway.
    (*iv*) 5 hours.
    (*v*) 385 kilometres
    (*vi*) Yes. A line chart.
    (*vii*) No. Histograms always have frequencies (how many?) on the vertical axis. This diagram has miles.

Unit 8 (*pp.* 20–21)
Answers to questions in the text
The Managing Director would use the mode.
The assistants would use the mean.
The fairest is the median.

Total wage bills: Factory *A* £7,200; *B* £8,000

Median wage in *F* £67·50
140 people work in *E*; 160 in *F*.

Answers to questions in the exercise
1.   (*a*) 6·25 (mean)   1 (mode)   6 (median)
    (*b*) 1002·4 (mean) 1002 (mode) 1002 (median)
    (*c*) 28·3 (mean)   21 (mode)   24 (median)
    (*d*) 111·25 (mean) 105 (mode) 111 (median)
2.   (*a*) mode
    (*b*) mean
    (*c*) median
    (*d*) median
3.   (*a*) 11875
    (*b*) 4·057
    (*c*) 4·8
        Use base other than zero.
4. 50·17 kg.

Unit 9 (*pp.* 22–23)
1. 2·2
2. Mean £2, same shape, mean 50p
3. 5·25 cm.
4. 10 years 6 months

Unit 10 (*p.* 25)
1. 170·05 cm.
3.   (*a*) 1750
    (*b*) 1500
    (*c*) £3854·5

Unit 11 (*p.* 27)
1. IQR Mathematics is approx. 20 (15–35)
IQR History is approx. 15 (21–36)
Median Mathematics is 24·5.
Median History is 28.
  (*a*) History.   (*b*) Both equal
2. Rainfalls in a short period of time only
3. Both zero (If one uses positive and negative differences).
  (*b*) This is unsatisfactory as a measure of variation from the mean, since the sum difference is always zero.

Unit 12 (*p.* 29)
1. Hanson $\sqrt{26·2}$, Brown $\sqrt{805}$
2. (*i*) $\sqrt{8·25}$ (*ii*) $\sqrt{8·25}$ (*iii*) $\sqrt{8·25}$;
when 10 added, no difference
3.   (*a*) Town *B*
    (*b*) Town *B*
4.   (*a*) 1·957
5. Mean 289 g.   S.D. = 10·7

Unit 13 (*p.* 31)
1.   (*i*) 1·74 m–1·86 m
    (*ii*) 1·787 m–1·813 m
    (*iii*) 23
    (*iv*) 477 men
2. Mean £3950, standard deviation £1125

Unit 13 (*continued*)
3. (*a*) 0·15%
   (*b*) 90—110
   (*c*) 2·3% or 23 in 1000

Unit 14 (*pp*. 32–3)
Answers to questions in the text
About ·15% of the tubes will last less than 1,680 hours.
No. Otherwise they would have no tubes to sell.
7·5 cm is the most common height of skirt above the knee in this sample.
Yes. There are more girls wearing skirts over 12·5 cm above the knee than there are wearing skirts below the knee.
The instrument with the smallest Standard Deviation is the most reliable.
The mean I.Q. of boys and girls is 100.
Some boys are brighter than any girl, but also some boys are duller than any girl. It is, in fact, very difficult to compare the whole population of boys and girls. The range of I.Q.s of boys is wider than that for girls, thus the distribution of I.Q.s for boys and girls is different.
Answers to questions in the exercises
2. If you add 10 to every make, the mean increases by 10 and the standard deviation stays the same. If you double every mark, the mean is double and so is the standard deviation.

Unit 15 (*p*. 35)
1. (*i*) Yes, steadily increasing.
   (*ii*) £4600 million
2. Hanson

Unit 16 (*p*. 38)
1. Miss Mann
2. (*a*) Puddleton 2·3,   Drydollop 2·8
   (*b*) 8.33, 5·95
   (*c*) Weighted average, takes account of age distribution of population.

Derived Statistics Problems (*pp*. 39–41)
1. (*i*) 40·25 kg
   (*ii*) 40·25 kg
2. (*i*) 50·70 kg
   (*ii*) 50·00 kg
   (*iii*) 50·57 kg
   (*iv*) 0·26% and 1·13%
3. (*a*) 167–170 cm (mode)
   (*b*) 167–170 cm (mean)
4. (*a*) £18.00 to £20.40
   (*b*) £20.50 to £22.90
5. (*i*) True
   (*ii*) False
   (*iii*) False
   (*iv*) False
   (*v*) True
6. 45 pupils passed; pass mark 24; median = 26; I.Q.R. = 17
7. 69, (*i*) 60 (*ii*) $\sqrt{435\cdot 4}$
8. (*i*) 9·0 m
   (*ii*) 0·114m
9. (*i*) 44
   (*ii*) $\sqrt{2\cdot 12}$
10. (*i*) 405 (*ii*) 414 (*iii*) 415 (*iv*) 418 (*v*) 420 (*vi*) 422 (*vii*) 429
    (*viii*) 434 (*ix*) 443 (*x*) 449 (*xi*) 463 (*xii*) 473 (*xiii*) 488
    No. of cars in 1965 = 2,316
11. (*a*) Pet Petrol
    (*b*) Troll Gass
    (*c*) Pet Petrol approx. 16%
    Troll Gass approx. 2½%

Unit 17 (*p*. 43)
1. (*i*) 1/4
   (*ii*) 17/100

Unit 18 (*pp*. 44–5)
Answers to questions in the exercises
Coin Tossing
1–4 Work out the practical probability using

$$\frac{\text{Total number of 3 heads}}{\substack{\text{Number of combined}\\ \text{tosses of 3 coins}}}, \quad \frac{\text{Total number of 2 heads}}{\substack{\text{Number of combined}\\ \text{tosses of 2 coins}}}, \text{etc}$$

Dice Rolling
1–4 Use a similar formula to the one above.
In Q. 4 each answer should be approximately the square of the preceding answer. The theoretical probabilities are 5/6, 25/36, 125/216.

Answers to the questions in the text
Spinning Tops
The probability of getting 6 is increased.
Flicking Matchsticks
The theoretical answer is 22/7 and you all know what that is!

Unit 19 (*p*. 47)
1. (*a*) 1/52
   (*b*) 1/13
   (*c*) 1/4
2. (*a*) 5/9
   (*b*) 4/9
   (*c*) 1
3. *Araby* 1/9,   *Gone With the Wind* 4/11,   *Go Fast* 1/3.

   Total probability = $\dfrac{4681}{3465}$ $>$ 1

Unit 20 (*p*. 49)
1. (*a*) 1/36
   (*b*) 1/12
   (*c*) 0
   (*d*) 2/9
   (*e*) 5/18
   (*f*) 7/12
   (*g*) 31/36
   (*h*) 11/12
2. Area 72 sq. cm, modal score 7.

Unit 21 (*p*. 52)
1. (*a*) 1/55
   (*b*) 28/55
   (*c*) 42/55
   (*d*) 4/55
2. (*a*) 16/81
   (*b*) 32/81
   (*c*) 8/27
   (*d*) 3
3. (*a*) 1/4
   (*b*) 1/64 (1/4)³
   (*c*) 27/64
   (*d*) 3 aircraft
4. At least £75

Probability Problems (*p*. 53)
1. (*b*) 1/8
   (*c*) 1/4
   (*d*) 15/16
   (*e*) 3/8
2. (*a*) 1/36   Most likely score = 7
   (*b*) 1/9   Probability = 1/6
   (*c*) 1/36
   (*d*) 0
3. (*a*) (*i*) 1/13
             (*ii*) 1/26
   (*b*) (*i*) 1/4
             (*ii*) 1/64
4. (*a*) 3/8
   (*b*) 3/14
   (*c*) 15/56
5. (*b*) 1/36
   (*c*) 1/3
6. 1/4, 8/11
7. 3/5, 1/2
8. (*a*) 0·65
   (*b*) 35
9. (*i*) 2/3
   (*ii*) 2/3
10. (*i*) 1/8
    (*ii*) 1/8
11. (*a*) 1/12   (*b*) 5/12
12. (*i*) 1/4
    (*ii*) 1/3
13. (*i*) 3/10
    (*ii*) 7/10
    (*iii*) 7/10
14. (*i*) 1/5
    (*ii*) 4/5
    (*iii*) 4 to 1

Revision Exercises (*p*. 55)
1. £3.00   2. £5.13
3. (*i*) 15 +   (*ii*) 19 +   (*iii*) 19 +
No one who is under the age of 16 is officially allowed to drive.
735. Approximately 45·9%.
The motor cyclist of 14 + years.
4. Approximately 70%.
0·998
(*i*) approx. 1/3
(*ii*) approx. 2/3
Approximately 80.
5. (*a*) 1/3 (*b*) 1/9, 1/27 (*c*) (1/3)⁸

Unit 22 (*p*. 59)
1. (*a*) 1/3
   (*b*) (*i*) 1/120 (*ii*) 3/40 (*iii*) 11/120 (*iv*) 1/6 (*v*) 99/120

4. (a) $\dfrac{1}{10^{15}}$ (b) $\dfrac{8}{10^{15}}$
or
(a) 0·000000000000001 (b) 0·000000000000008
This assumes he is the only one with two cards in the games.

5. (a) $\dfrac{24^2}{10^{10}}$ (b) $\dfrac{9 \times 24 \times 976}{10^{10}}$ (c) $\dfrac{976^2}{10^{10}}$
0·0000000576 0·0000046848 0·0000952576

6. (a) $\dfrac{1}{16 \times 10^5}^{2}$ or $\dfrac{1}{2,560,000,000}$

Unit 23 (p. 61)
*(This unit is difficult and may be omitted for many C.S.E. candidates.)
1. $F^4 + 4F^3S + 6F^2S^2 + 4FS^3 + S^4$
2. (i) 1 in both cases.
   (ii) 0·75 in both cases.
   (iii) $(F + S)^n$ is the binomial generating distribution, the nF is the mean number of failures, nFS the variance, and $\sqrt{nFS}$ the standard deviation.
3. 21/32. This may be calculated using 1 – probability of (no wrong answer), or, the longer way, using the distribution for right answers.
4. 2 packets has the highest probability ($6 \times (11)^2 \times (19)^2$). The machine was probably faulty.

Unit 24 (p. 63)
1. A random sample is one in which every item has the same chance of being selected.
2. (i) Sampling. Otherwise no tubes to use.
   (ii) Sampling. Because population changes every minute and it would be too time-consuming.
   (iii) The 'population' of all parachutes must be tested for safety reasons.
   (iv) The 'population' of reasons must be studied, or one may be accusing someone who was genuinely ill.
   (v) Sampling. Any other method would take too long.
3. (i) People who live in the capital may have different views from those of people living in the rest of Britain.
   (ii) The people who use London Airport are a special group usually above average in income, often much travelled.
   (iii) This excludes the thousands of non-telephone owners.
   (iv) This excludes the majority of people.
   (v) This is only a narrow age-range.
   (vi) One is more likely to be sampling Scots and Irish views (Macktosh, MacGregor, etc.).

Unit 25
Answers to Questions in the text (p. 64)
1. 11/243
2. 13·2%
3. 1·23
4. 1·67. '$n \times p$' of binomial generating distribution is $5 \times \frac{1}{3}$.
5. Total area represents total probability. Total probability is always 1 or 100% (in theory).
Total probability equals $\dfrac{\text{Total no. of occurrences}}{\text{Total no. of occurrences}}$ equals 1.
Answers to questions in the exercise (p. 66)
1. (a) 1/16, 15/16, 15/16 (b) 2
   (c) Bleak 4,600, Snowy 3,720

Unit 26 (p. 69)
1. Mean = $50 \times \frac{1}{2}$ = 25. S.D. = $\sqrt{50 \times \frac{1}{2} \times \frac{1}{2}} = \sqrt{12.5} = 3.5$
Approximately 0·15%. 35 would certainly exclude almost everybody who was simply guessing their answers.
2. Mean = 40. S.D. = $\sqrt{24}$
Three S.D.s below Mean is approximately 25.
Probability of interviewers only seeing 25 housewives who use the detergent is 0·15%.
Probability of interviewers seeing only 20 housewives who use the detergent is even less.
Thus either the original figure of 40% is wrong or the interviewer is lying.
3. 95·4%. The sample was not from this machine.

Unit 27 (p. 71)
1. (a) 0·6% = 2·4 'amps (b) 68·5% (= 274 lamps) 158·4 hours
2. 300
3. 60

Unit 28 (p. 75)
1. Dice

Probability and Sampling Problems (pp. 76–7)
1. (i) 1/16
   (ii) 3/8
   (iii) 11/16
2. (a) 5/16
   (b) 11/32
3. (b) 30
   (c) 400
   (d) 300
   (e) 3/8
6. ·01458 $= \dfrac{2 \times 3^6}{10^5}$, 18.
7. 11/32
8. (a) $\dfrac{3^{10}}{10^5}, \dfrac{5 \times 3^8}{10^5}, \dfrac{36}{104}$
9. (i) $\dfrac{6561}{10000}$ (ii) $\dfrac{729}{2500}$ (iii) $\dfrac{243}{5000}$ (iv) $\dfrac{9}{2500}$
   $\dfrac{1}{1000}$ Modal no. of failures, zero.
10. (i) $\left(\dfrac{1}{3}\right)^7$, (ii) $\left(\dfrac{2}{3}\right)^7$, (iii) $1 - \left(\dfrac{1}{3}\right)^7$.
    By expanding $\left(\dfrac{1}{3} + \dfrac{2}{3}\right)^7$
11. 0·023, negligible, 95·4%, 68·2%, 550 men.
12. (i) (a) 3·0%
       (b) 10·6%
       (c) 28·1%
       (d) 0·6%
    (ii) 93–107 approx.
13. (a) 78·7%
    (b) 2·3%

Unit 29 (p. 79)
1. (a) $y = 5x/100 + 2\frac{1}{2}$
   (b) $y = 4x$
   (c) $y = -12x/10 + 16$
   (d) $y = -x/32 + 2\frac{1}{2}$
2. 23·6 gallons

Unit 30 (p. 81)
1. Zero
2. 0
3. They both represent typical values of a distribution. Both use all items.
4. (a) $4y + 11x = 61$

Unit 32 (p. 85)
(a) negative
(b) negative
(c) positive
(d) positive
(e) positive
(f) zero
(g) positive
(h) negative
(i) positive
(j) negative

Unit 33 (p. 88)
1. (a) -0.57 (b) Yes (r > 0·5) (c) because it takes account of different methods of travel.
2. (a) Yes; No
   (b) $\frac{1}{2}$
   (c) Discrete

Collected Examples (pp. 89–93)
1. (a) The diagram is not labelled. The scale on the vertical axis is misleading.
   (b) The diagram is not labelled. The scale on the horizontal axis is misleading.
   (c) The use of different widths of bars is misleading.
   (d) The height of the cups represents the percentages. The absence of a vertical scale, together with the suggestion of volume of the cups as the measure, is very misleading.
2. (a) Line graph (dotted lines) (b) Histogram or Pie Chart.
3. (b) Approximately 55.
   (c) Most candidates score more than 50 marks. The distribution is therefore skewed negatively.

Collected Examples (*continued*)
4. (*d*) (*i*) 61   (*ii*) 26 (from 48 to 74)
5. (*a*) 14·68p
    (*b*) Between 13p and 15p
    (*c*) 15p
6. (*a*) 69   (*b*) 70·3
7. (*a*) 0·44%   (*b*) 4 or 5   (*c*) Approx. 1/227 (0·44%)
8. (*a*) (*i*) 1/32   (*ii*) 1/2
    (*b*) (*i*) Wrong. Because the possibilities are head, head: tail, tail: head, tail: and tail, head. The correct probability is therefore 2/4 or 1/2.
        (*ii*) Wrong. Head teachers, as a group, are older than the rest of the teaching profession. On these grounds alone they are likely to die sooner.
    (*c*) (*iii*) The ranges are approx. 70 to 130 and 85 to 115. The I.O.R.'s are approx. 93·3 to 106·7 and 96·7 to 103·3.
9. (*a*) A 51½   B 50½
    (*b*) A 35½   B 37½

10. The figures in order are.

10	10	40	40	150	150	200	200
20	20	80	80	300	300	400	400
40	40	160	160	600	600	800	800
40	40	160	160	600	600	800	800
110	110	440	440	1650	1650	2200	2200

Another important factor is whether the sample lived in rural areas, small towns or large cities.
11. (*i*) (*a*) indicates close agreement between two sets of data. This is a high positive correlation.
        (*b*) indicates little or no correlation.
        (*c*) indicates high negative correlation.
    (*ii*) (*a*) High positive correlation (very good agreement)
        (*b*) Insignificant correlation   (*c*) High negative correlation
12. (*b*) 45—60 mins   (*c*) No
    (*d*) Cumulative Frequency Distribution

Index